Buttons

FIELD GUIDE

Jill Gorski

Values and Identification

©2009 Krause Publications, Inc. a subsidiary of F+W Media, Inc.

Published by

krause publications

A subsidiary of F+W Media, Inc.

700 East State Street • Iola, WI 54990-0001
715-445-2214 • 888-457-2873
www.krausebooks.com

Our toll-free number to place an order or obtain
a free catalog is (800) 258-0929.

Library of Congress Control Number: 2008929068
ISBN-13: 978-0-89689-808-0
ISBN-10: 0-89689-808-3

Designed by Donna Mummery
Edited by Kristine Manty

On the cover: Buttons shown, clockwise from top right: small black glass, **$4**; small
brass twinkle, **$2**; small clear glass with painted back, **$3**; small blue glass, **$4**;
small blued steel, **$10**. Cover photo by Kris Kandler.

Printed in China

Dedication

To my loving, supportive and patient husband, Stephen. Bear, you are my rock!

Acknowledgments

I want to thank my family for riding the roller coaster with me.

I especially want to thank and acknowledge my friends in the Colorado State Button Society and the Colorado Springs Button Club for your encouragement, support, button loans, and your unbounded friendship.

In particular, I need to thank Susannah Jordan, president of the Colorado State Button Society. Sue, this book could never have been accomplished without your generous gifts of buttons, knowledge and, especially, time. I pray that I can be the friend and mentor to others that you have been to me.

Last, but certainly not least, thank you to Joe Kertzman and Kristine Manty at Krause Publications. Joe, thank you for your vision and support. Kris, thank you for cracking the whip!

Contents

A Brief History of the Button

It's not difficult to recognize buttons as miniature works of art. They can be simple, as seen in a faceted black glass button, or they can be elaborate, as in a carved Bethlehem pearl button. What many people don't realize is how much history can be gleaned from the study of buttons.

Buttons, as we know them, are not as old as you would think. While button-like objects have been found throughout all human history, they were generally used as ornamentation or jewelry. This all changed when crusaders brought home samples of buttons and buttonholes from the Middle East in the 13th Century. In order to realize how the button has evolved to its present day purpose, we need to revisit the progression of the Industrial Revolution.

European Crafts Guilds were created around the year 1250 A.D. in order to organize craftsmen and artisans. One of these guilds was for buttonmakers. Guild members dictated the trends of the day and their work was truly incredible, with an emphasis on quality. Buttons were marked and records were kept, documenting each artisan's craft. At this point in history, buttons were jewels made in sets to be attached and removed each time the garment was worn. Artisans created stunning sets for the elite, crafting one button at a time, and using materials such as gold and silver set with jewels. Documents and letters from this time period tell of staggering sums of money being spent on buttons. Buttons have been found buried with prized jewelry, bequeathed in wills, and listed in household inventories. Royalty commissioned artists to make their buttons and kings adorned their garments with as many buttons as possible in order to show their superiority over another ruler; the old "he with the most buttons, wins!"

While the aristocracy enjoyed magnificent buttons, the common man wore buttons made of materials such as cloth, wood, bone, and leather. This was due, in part, to the prohibitive cost, but also due to a royal decree that dictated what the lower class could and could not wear. Buttons told society where you ranked on the social ladder.

By the 17th and 18th centuries, buttons were being made in a wide variety of materials and styles. France and England were the centers of industry. Artisans branched out and had very profitable sidelines making buttons. Weavers made woven buttons, potters made ceramic buttons, and so forth. Buttons increased in size and opulence. Activities of the day were often depicted on these buttons, like little history books for us to study. For the most part, buttons were mainly made for men's clothing. Waistcoats, shirts and outer coats were covered with beautiful buttons, as many as 24 in a set. In addition to clothing, buttons were also used to fasten shoes and gloves. This means collectors today have a plethora of lovely buttons to collect.

American manufacturers had also begun making fine buttons; however, the majority was still being imported from England. As talk of revolution grew, it became increasingly patriotic to wear only American-made buttons. Many patriotic craftsmen manufactured buttons made from wood, pewter, brass, and papier mâché in addition to their main craft. Phineas Pratt, a well-known manufacturer of piano keys, began making buttons from ivory. Patriot silversmith Paul Revere is said to have produced fine silver buttons.

As the Industrial Revolution progressed, demand for everyday objects like cloth and buttons grew. In America and Europe, factories began to produce many fine buttons in quantities not previously possible. Some of the finest buttons ever manufactured were crafted during the "Golden Age" of button making (in America; 1830-1850). Gilt buttons were crafted during this period. They were made using a mix of manufacturing methods and hand craftsmanship that produced a button of superior quality, not seen before. Gilt buttons were first made in England but America was quick to learn the process. Sporting, military, and livery buttons made during this period are very collectable.

In addition to an increase in mass-production, new types of materials were being discovered. Hard rubber was introduced by the Goodyear brothers in 1849. The U.S. Navy used rubber buttons due to their durability. Leo Baekeland created the first true plastic in 1909. Bakelite, his creation, was used to make everything from buttons to telephones. In the 1920s, a German chemist, Herman Staudinger, studied the molecular makeup of plastics and was the first to use the term "polymers." In the 1930s and 1940s, glass and plastic novelty buttons depicted every object imaginable. Shell and China buttons were also popular. China buttons, some with stenciled patterns on them, were an alternative to cloth buttons that wore out before the garment did. The majority of buttons purchased now were for use on women's and children's clothing. Unfortunately, progress, as we know, can be a two-edged sword. The Industrial Revolution that had been such a boon to the button industry now sent it into decline. Buttons were mass-produced as simply and cheaply as possible. What many people today picture in their mind as a button is the result of all this progress: a common, white shirt button, small and inconsequential.

Fortunately, for all of us, there are still artisans who believe beautiful buttons should be available for everyone to enjoy and treasure. Button clubs, such as the National Button Society, formed in 1938, have fought to preserve the integrity of buttons as historical artifacts and they have done a wonderful job of enlisting those who dictate button fashion. Thanks to the efforts of clubs and individual collectors, button collecting is alive and well all over the world.

Introduction

Why collect buttons?

Humans, by nature, are collectors. The reasons may differ, but the results are the same: the more, the better! As is true of most collectibles, they connect us to fond memories; sometimes personal, sometimes historical.

Buttons have a universal appeal. Not only are buttons small, plentiful and portable, but they are very affordable. Buttons can be found for pennies a piece so your collection can grow quickly, or you can easily use them as an addition to any other type of collection. Buttons depicting bears might be collected by teddy bear collectors, while buttons made from Bakelite would be a lovely addition to a Bakelite jewelry collection. People all over the world collect buttons. There is such a wide variety of types and styles that no two people would have the same collection.

Given the familiarity of such a simple, every day object, it would be easy to think that collecting buttons might quickly prove to be a boring pursuit. Let me assure you that the opposite is, in fact, true and I hope that this book will, if nothing else, cause you to never look at a button in quite the same way ever again.

What to collect

Deciding what types of buttons to collect may be the most difficult task a collector faces. Here are some questions that may help you decide:

* Are buttons your primary collection, or an addition to another collection?

* Would you like to enter competitions with your collection?

* Are you planning to sell or trade your buttons?

* Would you like to display or craft with your buttons?

Considering how your buttons will be used will be helpful. Regardless of how you answered these questions there are buttons out there for you. In general, variety is extremely desirable, even if you decide to specialize in one or two types of buttons, and especially if you choose to compete. A mix of sizes, shapes, designs, and other material embellishments (OMEs) is best. My best advice is to collect what you love, first and foremost. I promise you'll never be disappointed!

Where to find great buttons

The first thing that needs to be said here is that ALL BUTTONS ARE GREAT and any find is a good find. One of the first questions that I am asked is,

"Where do you find all your buttons?" I used to say "everywhere," but the truth is, I get most of my buttons from people, perhaps like you, who know I collect buttons and have bags, jars, and boxes at home filled with buttons (often their grandmothers').

They really have no idea what they have. Sometimes I am able to show them what treasures they have and they take them back home with a smile on their face. On occasion, however, they feel that the buttons would have a better home with someone who will love them, and I am able to add to my collection, as well as preserve history, often for no cost at all!

The moral here is: tell everyone you know that you are looking for buttons. Be prepared for puzzled looks on their faces. "Buttons?" they will ask. "Like, buttons? Really?" They might even laugh. But you needn't worry; you'll be the one chuckling when you pull out fabulous finds, knowing what they are really worth.

Here are some ideas of places to begin your search:

- Family and friends
- Fabric stores
- Antiques dealers
- Flea markets
- Estate sales
- Yard sales

- Thrift stores
- On-line sales, like eBay
- Local and state sponsored button shows
- Other button collectors
- Don't forget to look on clothing at the thrift stores and yard sales, not just in bags and jars
- Button auctions (several companies specialize in these)

While you can certainly find buttons at these locations, you may also discover that the prices they are asking are not only more than you want to pay, but based on unsupported assumptions. That's why it's important to educate yourself. It is my hope that this book will start you on that path.

A word about prices

A little knowledge can be a dangerous thing, so the saying goes, and it can be true with button collecting. It's easy to go to, say, a flea market and want to purchase every old Mason jar of buttons you see. Something I found helpful when I first started collecting was to set a budget. For example, I made a rule that I would not pay more than $1 for a glass button, and no more than $5 for a large jar of buttons. I was able to find many great buttons in those $5 (or less) jars, often worth much more than the price I paid. In addition, I had great specimens to study while I was learning.

There are some fabulous buttons to be found that cost much more than $1 and they are worth every penny. I will always remember my first major purchase. It was a pewter button made by the Battersea Company and it was $25! I thought I would faint as I handed over the money, but I reassured myself that this was a good addition to my collection, with the knowledge that I had researched buttons made by Battersea, and I was purchasing it from a well-respected button collector. It remains one of my favorite buttons to this day. I now seek out more from the same maker, when I can afford to.

These two examples demonstrate two schools of thought when it comes to collecting. The first example would be to spend a little, collect a lot, regardless of the type of button. This works well and is the method I used when I was learning about buttons. It gives you a wide variety of study samples, as well as stock to trade or sell later to upgrade your collection. The second example will build your collection slowly, but you will have magnificent buttons if you do your homework. Be warned: once you decide to collect buttons, you will find them, seemingly, everywhere you look and it is very easy to get carried away…hmmm, and this is bad, how?

My purpose in writing this Field Guide is two-fold:

1. To encourage button collecting and preservation.
2. To give button enthusiasts a simple and portable reference.

The prices in this guide are supplied in order to give you an educated reference. Prices have been determined to the best of my professional ability after consulting with other professionals. Many factors affect button prices, some of which include the condition of the button, as well as what buttons might be needed for state or national competitions (known as Awards, and published online and in the NBS Bulletin). Where or from whom you purchase can affect pricing. A vendor's knowledge and overhead costs can affect what you pay for your buttons. There are always supply and demand issues as well. Buttons are a popular collectible and many people are taking advantage of this by adding buttons to their inventory. Perhaps you are one of these people. I'm glad that you wish to educate yourself about your product. There is nothing more aggravating to a button collector than to see a small bag of 15-cent shirt buttons priced at $5, simply because they know buttons are popular with collectors.

Education is the key to an enjoyable collection and this book encompasses only a small portion of the information available about buttons. I encourage you to talk, listen, read, and learn about buttons whenever and wherever possible.

General Tips

Helpful tools to carry

There are several tools that you will find indispensable in your quest for great buttons. I keep a small cosmetics bag with me filled with the following:

- A good magnifying glass. The stronger the better, but it needn't be large. Many collectors use a jewelers' loop.

- A small magnet. This will help you identify metal buttons.

- A very soft, child's toothbrush. Most buttons can be cleaned with just a gentle brush. More will be discussed in a future chapter.

- A small cleaning cloth. I like to carry a small cloth that might be used to clean eyeglasses in my kit. This cloth can be used to keep oils from your fingers off the buttons, as well as a place to lay your button for examination. I also keep a jewelry polishing cloth at home.

There are other tools available for collectors, such as measuring devices, cleaning pastes and more specialized tools. I will discuss these in future chapters.

Identifying your buttons

For such a simple object, a button has a lengthy list of parts and identifiers. The front of a button is lovely and catches our attention right away, like a pretty face. We all know, however, that there's more to beauty than meets the eye. The back of a button tells us more about a button's character, where it's been, the life it's led.

In the chapters to follow, I will discuss each type of button by its material makeup, construction, and characteristic features. You will see fronts and backs of buttons with descriptions and a suggested average price for each. In addition, I'll give you tips for cleaning your buttons. There are several general areas I'd like to discuss in this overview.

Button sizes

Button manufacturers used a French system of measuring buttons called "lignes" (lines). You may find this number imprinted, written or on a sticker on a button back. Carded buttons, especially newer ones, will have a button size listed on the card. This was usually shown as inches. As an aid to identification, I list button size, when relevant, using the system developed by the NBS. There are two types of measuring devices available to collectors for this purpose. This system sizes a button as:

- Diminutive: up to 3/8 inch
- Small: from 3/8 to 3/4 inch
- Medium: from 3/4 to 1-1/4 inch
- Large: from 1-1/4 inch and up

It is interesting to note the sizes with regard to a single button:

This button is small = 1/2" = 12.7mm = 20 lignes.

When you have two identical buttons of different sizes, they are referred to as "Mother/Daughter." Here are three identical buttons of graduating size. The smallest measures 1/2 inch and largest is 7/8 inch. Grandmother/Mother/Daughter?

Button shanks

A button is attached to a garment in one of two ways. A button with holes front to back is called a "sew-through." A button with a device on the back, such as a metal plate and loop, is called a shank.

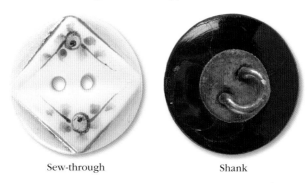

Sew-through   Shank

Some back types are typical to certain button types. I show and explain these in detail within the appropriate chapters. One interesting and fun type of construction is found on sew-through buttons called whistle buttons. Notice that there is one small hole on the top of the button, but turn it over and you will find two holes.

Look straight through...you should be able to see a small portion of the two holes through the top hole. Whistles come in all shapes, sizes, and many materials. These are black glass buttons.

These three whistle buttons are also black glass.

These two plastic buttons both appear to be whistles, but on closer inspection, only the black button is a true whistle. The top hole on the pink button is too large and allows you to see nearly all of the bottom holes. The black button also has pearl inlay on the face.

The back of this medium black glass button reveals a broken shank. This may decrease the value slightly, but this button is still collectible. Collectors use a device called a "spider" to hold the button for display. Note as well that this button has a "back mark": "LeChic" is the name of the button line by B. Blumenthal Co.

Back marks

One way to identify a button is through the marks on the back. These marks include maker's name, brand, patent, quality mark, etc. They can be verbal or pictorial in nature. You will see several back marks identified on buttons in this book. Here are a few:

This plain little fabric-covered button holds a fabulous secret on the back: it was manufactured in Paris, France, probably in the early 1800s.

The back mark of the fabric-covered button reads, "TRESSE DE PARIS." A "Paris Back," as this is called, is one of the most popular and collectible buttons out there. It also has a pad or cloth shank.

This sew-through wooden button has a beautiful design carved on the front. It is also a Paris back.

The back of this button is marked "L.CJ" and "CAEN"; two small stars and two other tiny marks appear to be here, perhaps a maker's mark?

This brass button
appears utilitarian, until
you turn it over...

The back is leather.
The mark reads,
"PARIS/a star/
SOLIDITE/a crest."

At first glance, it is not obvious what material this button is made of. One look at the back mark, however, immediately identifies it as rubber.

The back of the rubber button says, "N.R. Co. Goodyear's P=T.," and is one of several back marks used by the Goodyear Co. (see Rubber chapter for more information). The shank style is termed a pin shank.

This large (1-1/2") composition button (see Plastics) has a patent date back mark, shown on the following page.

The back mark reads, "PATENTED/NOV 25, 1919." It is important to note that a patent date is not necessarily the date that the button was manufactured.

This appears to be a U.S. Navy uniform button.

The back mark reads, "R&W Robinson" inside of a banner. This back mark was used by the Robinson Company from 1836-1848, telling us when this button was made. Also note the thicker, heavy brass shank, common on older buttons.

The pattern on this button suggests a dyed leather button.

The back mark reads, "Canadian Buttons Limited." This company, founded in 1884, is still in existence today. It manufactures plastic injection products, giving us an insight into how this button is made.

One last word about button backs:

You may find a button with a small hole in the back. This is not a back mark. A "pick" mark is a mark left in a horn button to lift it from the mold. This mark is often slightly irregular.

If the hole is small and "perfect," it is likely a hole left by a "hot needle." A hot needle is used by experienced collectors to test materials.

Beware of imitations

Many times buttons are erroneously labeled, as illustrated by the picture on P. 38. These "logger buttons," as they are labeled, were a fun souvenir from a trip to Alaska.

On closer inspection, however, it is clear that they are a type of snap or stud used on overalls. While I consider them a great addition to my collection, they are not actually buttons.

Materials are often mislabeled on carded buttons. Be wary if a button is labeled as "natural material." This does not mean it is a completely natural button. Another famous misnomer are old black glass buttons labeled as "jet."

Black glass buttons were developed as an alternative to jet buttons, which were expensive and custom made for the upper classes. Queen Victoria started the craze when she took to wearing black

These aren't buttons at all; they're a type of snap or stud.

mourning clothing, with black jet buttons, after the death of her husband, Prince Albert. Her subjects were so moved that they took to imitating her style of dress to honor her. True jet is a mineral and very rare. Many other material imitations exist so it is wise to be certain when purchasing a more pricey button.

From the front, this
looks like a U.S. Air
Force button, but as you
can see from the back, it is
a screw-type stud.

Bringing your buttons home

Let's pretend you've just come home after a wonderful day at the flea market. You couldn't resist that old tin full of buttons for only $4.

You decide to sit down at the kitchen table and see what treasures await you inside the tin. It would feel so lovely to run your hands through those buttons; such a hypnotic feeling! But wait! It's an odd fact, but a fact nonetheless, that all manner of objects are in that tin with your buttons.

I have found sewing needles, nails, pins and staples, to name a few of the sharp objects that might await you.

Not all of the odd items are sharp though. One of my latest finds was a tax token. Not knowing what a tax token was, I looked it up and got a history lesson: tax tokens resemble coins and were issued by 12 different states (Alabama, Arizona, Colorado, Illinois, Kansas, Louisiana, Mississippi, Missouri, New Mexico, Oklahoma, Utah, and Washington state).

Tokens can be made of aluminum, copper, zinc, brass, plastic (in several colors), fiber, cardboard and paper; 1 and 5 mills are the most common denominations, but other denominations include: 1/5 cent, 1-1/2 mills, and "tax on 10c or less." Pretty cool!

OK, so you dump your buttons into a cake pan that you line with a dish towel. This is so you won't break or chip any of your buttons and to keep them from jumping off the table.

You begin to poke through your treasure, being sure to look at the backs of them (of course). After an initial look-see, you may feel the urge to separate your buttons by material or any other method you choose.

I find it useful to use paper bowls, so I can stack them later if I get interrupted by my hungry family.

On my first go-through, I try to pull out pearl buttons, glass buttons, plastic buttons, and metal buttons. I often find I need a bowl for "special" buttons, too.

Some buttons may be in poor condition. Many older buttons are made from organic materials, like pearl, or a mix of organic and chemicals, like celluloid. Look at the button on the next page:

This celluloid button was crumbling when I found it and took no encouragement at all to fall apart in my hand! It is important to keep these buttons separated from your other buttons. I advise you to throw out those that are rusted, green, or decayed to a great degree. The fact that your flea market buttons were stored in a tin increases the likelihood that you may find buttons in similar condition. Buttons need to breathe! If you choose to keep your collection in a container, including plastic bags, you may want to either leave the lid loose, or "play with" your buttons often. Consider showing them off in candy dishes, candle holders, or pretty bowls. I heartily encourage you to use and enjoy your buttons on a daily basis, and don't just store them away for another generation to find.

The celluloid button fallen apart. Note the typical "omega"-shape shank in the upper part of the picture.

Collectors find it handy to mount their buttons on acid-free matte board for storage and organizing. This type of board is available at framing and craft stores. An awl or ice pick can be used to make a hole in the board. Make the hole large enough so that the button sits flush on the board (if possible) and hold it in place with a coated wire that is slipped through the holes or shank and twisted. Top loading plastic sleeves are also available, so that you don't scratch your buttons when storing them. Large plastic food-storage bags also work well, if you leave them open at the top.

Remember those buttons I told you to throw out? Consider using them to learn how to clean your buttons properly. Most buttons don't need to be cleaned with anything other than a clean, dry, soft cloth. If your buttons have any kind of finish on them, such as paint or luster, be careful not to rub these delicate finishes right off your button. Each chapter will give you basic care and cleaning directions for that particular type of button. As a general rule, do not put your buttons in water. "But wait," people say. "I can wash my clothes with the buttons on them, so why can't I use water on them?" I will explain this in subsequent chapters. For now, I ask that you trust me on this one!

Another consideration for your collection is whether to keep records. Most people, at first, do not keep any record of where they purchased their buttons or the price they paid for them. Most people don't need to. I know I didn't keep records at first, but now I wish I had. Your system can be as simple or as detailed as you think it needs to be. You may even start with one method and find you need to change it as you expand your collection, or begin selling and trading buttons. It's also a fantastic learning tool. It gives you a reference button to compare other buttons to that you may find in your travels. Believe me, this is a great tool when you are first learning, to have the actual button to examine close up. Pictures can only do so much. At first I wrote the information on the back of the card where I stored the button, but if I wanted to move that button, I lost the information, or had to transfer it as well. Many collectors use a numbering system. You may see pictures in this book where a tiny number has been written on a sticker and put on the button back. My favorite system is to either photograph or scan my button cards and make notes in the computer or on the sheets I print out and keep in a notebook. Whichever method you use, I feel it is worth your time to keep records.

Five small Mother of Pearl (MOP) shirt buttons (one missing), 1930s to 1940s, buttons have fisheye and rimmed design, attached to card with wire, "Ultra Kraft," **$2**. The little girl on the card appeared in variation for many years. It's fun to note the original price tag at upper right.

Carded Buttons

Are buttons on the original cards worth more? Most serious collectors are not particularly interested in carded buttons, because you would not be able to use them in competition on the cards.

Many people who collect carded buttons do so primarily for the card, and secondly for the button, so condition would be important.

They make lovely display pieces in frames or even in a scrapbook. I would ask myself what the buttons are worth and base my price on that.

Bottom line: if you like them, collect them.

Four medium pink, molded plastic Prevue buttons, 1940s, **$3**. The guarantee, "These buttons are authentic for the latest styles and patterns," makes reference to the existence of ready-made paper patterns newly available in stores (Butterick was first).

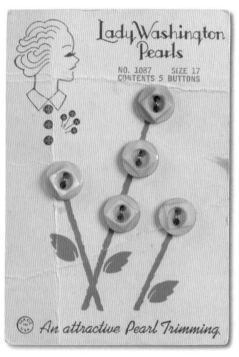

Five small carved and dyed MOP shirt buttons, Lady
Washington Pearls, early to mid-1900s, **$3**. Carded Pearl buttons
are plentiful, so condition of card should determine price. The
color of these is very nice.

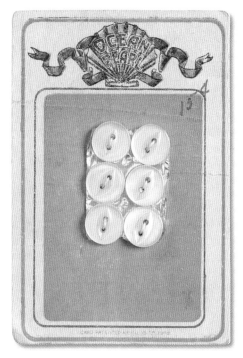

Six small natural color MOP buttons, fisheye design, Ocean Pearl, early 1900s, **$2**. The card says "patented April 15th 1919," but a patent date does *not* mean a manufacture date, but they certainly can help with the dating process.

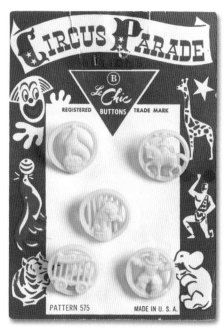

Set of five yellow, molded plastic "Circus Parade Buttons," LeChic Buttons (B. Blumenthal Co.), 1930s, **$25**. Sets can be found off the original cards for about $15. Make sure they are all the same color and a complete set (see glossary). Original cards in excellent condition are difficult to find. Fun sets like this are highly collectible.

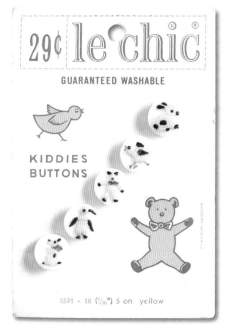

Set of five small, white glass "Kiddie Buttons," with yellow animal themes, le chic, 1930s, **$25**. Sold for children's clothing, there were many theme variations of these sets. Individual buttons are easy to find and cost about $1 each. Sets must be the same color and group and can be found off cards for about $15.

Twenty-four small, one-piece French metal buttons, stamped leaf design with enamel, possibly early 1800s, excellent condition for age of the card, **$35**. Réposé refers to a method of design construction that involves hammering from the reverse side, however it also refers to a two-piece construction, and these buttons are one piece.

Eight small, one-piece, wooden modified ball-shape buttons, self shank, grid design stamped into top, sewn on card, possibly early 1900s, **$15**. Backs have a knob-shaped shank that has been flattened and the hole drilled through for sewing. The lovely workmanship on these buttons adds to the value of the card.

Ceramics

Ceramics is a general term and any button made from natural clay would be classified as such. Here we will discuss china, porcelain and jasperware, a type of stoneware. Others not shown here include pottery types such as Satsuma, Norwalk and Delft; Wedgwood also made stoneware buttons.

Some ceramic buttons, such as chinas, may bear a likeness to glass. Both will feel cold on your cheek, but china button backs will have a gritty look to them where they rested while being fired. Ceramic buttons will often look "gritty," especially under a magnifying glass. Ceramic buttons tend to be sew-throughs.

Because of its porous nature, ceramic buttons should not be cleaned with water, unless you are certain that they have been sealed and fired.

China buttons are a popular type of button. Calico china buttons were made to match fabrics of the period and can be found in over 325 different documented patterns. Stenciled china buttons have a hand-painted (later sprayed on) design. These have also been catalogued and you may find numbers referenced with some patterns, referring to the documentation. Many collectors have cards with each pattern printed on them and a quest to find one of each pattern, size and color. I liken it to filling a bingo card, and just as much fun. The NBS has a publication available the gives a complete list and guidelines for collecting china buttons.

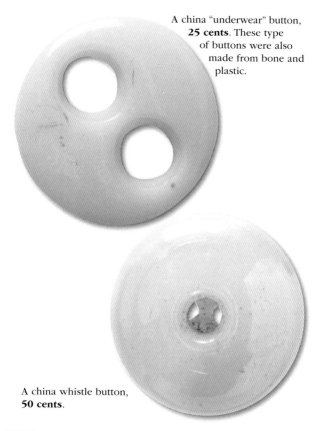

A china "underwear" button, **25 cents**. These type of buttons were also made from bone and plastic.

A china whistle button, **50 cents**.

Small china button, smooth white top with green band, late 1800s, shank style is called a "bird cage," two-piece construction, **$5**.

Typical small china buttons, **50 cents**. China buttons were made in the 1840s in France, England and New York. They were the plastic shirt button of their day due to their sturdy nature. The backs of the china buttons are shown at right. Note the rough-looking centers where the sew-through holes are.

Various sizes of china
shoe buttons.

China "gaiter," small, loop
and plate shank, bullseye
pattern, **$3**.

China "gaiter," small,
loop and plate shank,
shape #4, **$1.50**.

Assorted china buttons, small, two- and four-hole sew-through, late 1800s, **$2-$4**. The gray color was mixed into the china prior to firing. The dark brown to the right of it has an iridescent luster. The dark orange, brown and green are painted, front and back.

China, small, four-hole sew-through, front and backs shown, banded colors, "dish" style, **50 cents**.

China buttons, small, four-hole sew-through, late 1800s, "pie crust" design, lines radiate from the center but there is a raised rim at the center and outer edge, **$2** each. The blue finish on the one at top is paint.

China buttons, small, four-hole sew-through, late 1800s, "radiating line" design, **$2** each. The red finish on the one at top is paint.

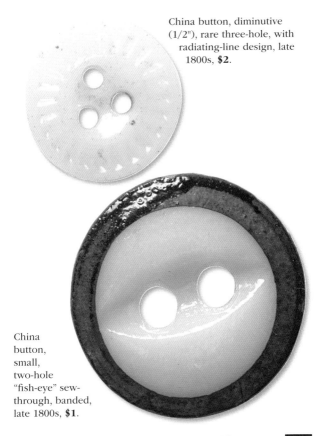

China button, diminutive (1/2"), rare three-hole, with radiating-line design, late 1800s, **$2**.

China button, small, two-hole "fish-eye" sew-through, banded, late 1800s, **$1**.

China, small, four-hole sew-through, banded "inkwell," **$1**.

China button, small, four-hole sew-through, border has a "Hobnail" design, late 1800s, **$1**.

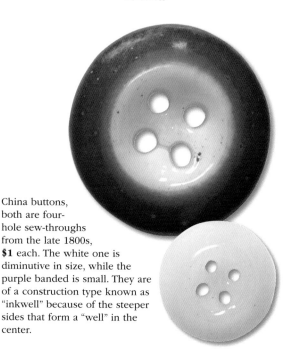

China buttons, both are four-hole sew-throughs from the late 1800s, **$1** each. The white one is diminutive in size, while the purple banded is small. They are of a construction type known as "inkwell" because of the steeper sides that form a "well" in the center.

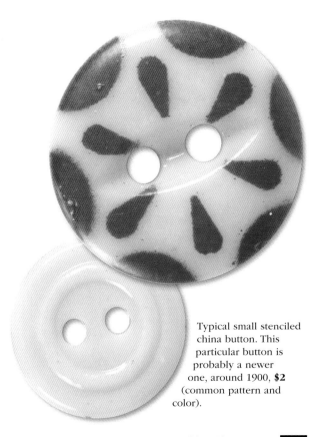

Typical small stenciled china button. This particular button is probably a newer one, around 1900, **$2** (common pattern and color).

Stenciled china, small, two-hole sew-through, late 1800s, **$2-$4**.

Stenciled china, small, two-hole sew-through, late 1800s, **$2-$4**.

Stenciled china, small, two-hole sew-through, late 1800s, **$2**.

Stenciled china, small, two-hole sew-through, late 1800s, **$2** for round; **$6** for square shape.

More small stenciled chinas; the face is especially fun and is pattern #29, **$2-$5**.

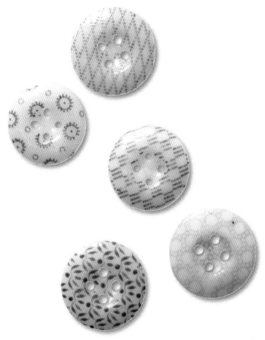

Calico chinas, small, four-hole sew-through, late 1800s, various calico patterns and colors, **$3-$5**.

Calico chinas, small, most are four-hole sew-throughs, late 1800s, various calico patterns in shades of brown, **$3-$10** each, depending on rarity of pattern.

Porcelain button, self-shank, painted front, 1800s, **$4**.

Porcelain button, self-shank, painted front, probably early 1900s, $4.

Porcelain button, small, applied plastic shank, hand-painted rabbit by artist Cindy Webb, 2007, **$4**.

Porcelain button, self-shank, small, hand-painted, early 1800s, **$7**.

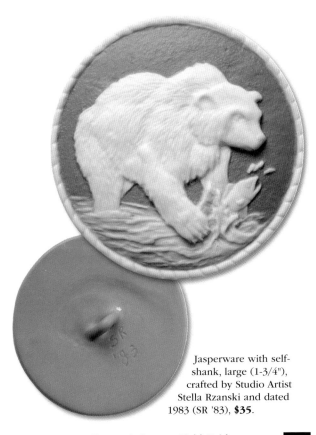

Jasperware with self-shank, large (1-3/4"), crafted by Studio Artist Stella Rzanski and dated 1983 (SR '83), **$35**.

Fabric

Fabric buttons include fabric stretched over metal and wooden molds, as well as buttons made from woven or worked threads.

They come in all sizes. I even have a crocheted button that measures 3/16". Many have incredible workmanship, yet they are highly undervalued in today's market.

Because the fibers in fabric can be very brittle (it is organic, after all), never brush or treat fabric buttons with any force. If you must clean your fabric, you can use a dab of dry cleaning fluid.

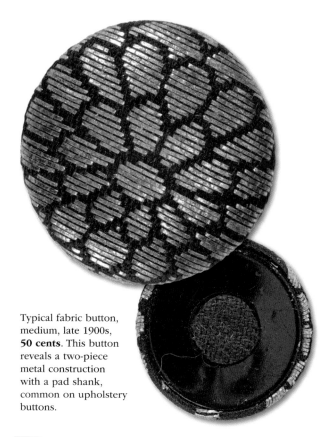

Typical fabric button, medium, late 1900s, **50 cents**. This button reveals a two-piece metal construction with a pad shank, common on upholstery buttons.

Beaded button, medium, late 1900s, **$1**. The beads on this button were worked on fabric that covers a two-piece plastic mold with self shank. The back is marked "36." In this case, it does not refer to the ligne number.

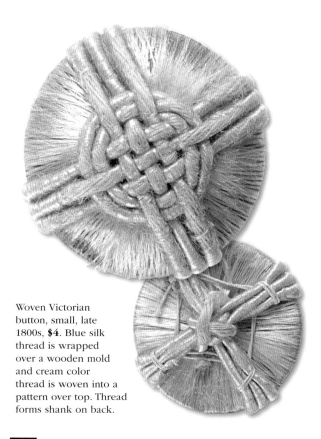

Woven Victorian
button, small, late
1800s, **$4**. Blue silk
thread is wrapped
over a wooden mold
and cream color
thread is woven into a
pattern over top. Thread
forms shank on back.

Woven Victorian button, medium, late 1800s, **$5**. Silk thread was used to cover the mold and then the pattern, known as Victorian Flag, was woven over the top. The back of the button shows a thread shank.

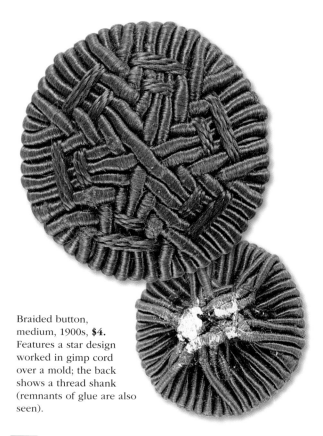

Braided button, medium, 1900s, **$4.** Features a star design worked in gimp cord over a mold; the back shows a thread shank (remnants of glue are also seen).

Braided button, medium, 1900s, **$4**. Uses a soutache cord woven in a basket weave pattern over a mold; this button has a metal loop shank.

Crocheted button,
medium, **$3**. Cream-
colored button is
a circular crochet
pattern, worked off
the mold; the back
reveals a wooden
ring mold. Crochet is
stretched over and the
thread back is created by
pulling the sides together.

Crocheted button, small, crocheted over mold, thread shank, early 1900s, **$2**.

Crocheted button,
medium, vine crochet
worked with metal
ring center and over
mold, metal loop shank,
early 1900s, **$3**.

Glass

Glass buttons are probably the most plentiful, and, in my opinion, beautiful buttons available.

Because of this, glass is a great and inexpensive place to start your button collection. You could even specialize in it and keep expanding your collection for many years to come.

Prior to World War II, America was supplied with glass buttons from Czechoslovakia. After WWII, there was a shift

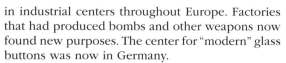

in industrial centers throughout Europe. Factories that had produced bombs and other weapons now found new purposes. The center for "modern" glass buttons was now in Germany.

By 1969, however, plastics were a more profitable commodity, and the supply of German glass buttons dwindled.

Recently, the market has been seeing more and more "new Czech" glass buttons.

For purposes of dating the buttons in this chapter, the following are used in regards to the era they were most probably created:

- Old: prior to 1940
- Modern: 1940-1960
- New: after 1960

There are a number of materials that can imitate glass. I use two common tests for glass.

First, glass is cool on your cheek, but so is china. Tap your button on your teeth. If you hear

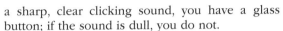

a sharp, clear clicking sound, you have a glass button; if the sound is dull, you do not.

This can take a little practice, but use a known glass button and compare its sound if need be.

Glass comes in a variety of colors, finishes, shapes and sizes. Most books, including the NBS classification book, divide glass into two sections: black (BG) and colored (CG). I have divided the chapter the same way, but because they have many of the same characteristics, they are discussed as one type here.

Glass color is not always as easy to discern as you would think. Look at these pictures on the following two pages:

These buttons appear to be blue, iridescent, gold, and green. Turn them over, and...

Blue is now black. Iridescent is clear. Gold is black, and the green is...well, that's a longer story I'll discuss later.

There are a number of DFs (decorative finishes) that are applied to glass buttons. They include paint, gold, silver, bronze, and aurora lusters, and back finishes such as mercury and mirror.

Beside DFs, glass buttons have some of the most interesting and numerous back types of any button material. Here are a few you will find:

This is one type of self-shank.

These are two other types of self-shanks.

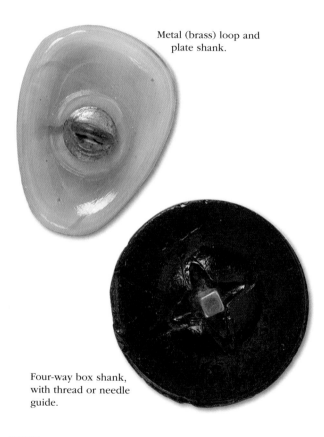

Metal (brass) loop and plate shank.

Four-way box shank, with thread or needle guide.

Metal rosette shank.

Whistle and sew-through buttons are available in glass also.

Not pictured here is a "swirl back." You will be able to see where the metal shank was inserted into the hot glass and turned into the glass like a corkscrew. It leaves a ripple effect in the glass as it cools.

Glass is such a wonderful medium for design work. There are many construction, as well as surface design, methods that can be used for glass buttons. I will not list them all here, but I will reference as many as possible in the photos. Glass buttons can have other material embellishments (OME) *on* them, or can *be* the OME on a button. The possibilities are seemingly endless when it comes to glass buttons.

Black glass

Both of these are
BG whistles, small,
modern, with gold luster
accents, **$2** each.

More BG whistles, small, modern, with gold luster accents, **$2** each.

These buttons
have wonderful
shapes, other than
round, for you to
enjoy. Both are
small in size and
have self-shanks, are
modern, and the heart
also has a lovely pressed
design, **$2-$3** each.

These are two other buttons with wonderful shapes. Both are small, have self-shanks, gold luster, and are modern, **$2-$3** each.

BG flower shape, small, "lacy-like" surface design formed by pressing glass into handmade molds, old, four-way box shank, **$15**. This is one of my favorite buttons.

Black glass, medium, self-shank, modern, molded and faceted
shamrock design, **$10**.

Black glass, large (2-1/8"), four-way box shank, old, **$7**.

Black glass, medium, four-way box shank, satin finish, Art-Nouveau style Iris with raised flower center, old, **$4**.

BG, small, metal loop
shank, one piece,
pierced, old, **$12**. This
in an incredible button;
the raised center is
etched with tiny rings of
pattern, with gold luster.
The outer ring resembles
cut steel pieces. Imagine a
row of these on a ladies dress!
Who needs jewelry?

BG, medium, four-way box
shank, pressed mold design,
old, **$4**.

BG, small, brass loop and plate shank, dull finish, old, **$12**.
This "pictorial" button is titled "Stag Hunt." Many sizes and
versions were produced. It depicts a hunter with a coiled
horn and his dogs in the foreground, and the fleeing stag in
the distance. The amount of detail on a button so small is
incredible!

These old and small BG buttons seem very plain; one is polished, and one is faceted…

The backs, however, are wonderful! The top button has a rosette shank. The bottom button has a four-way box shank, **$1-$2** each.

BG, small, metal loop and plate shank, modern, **$2**.

BG, small, faceted ball
with metal shank, possibly
old, **$1**.

Two
BG, small,
self-shanks,
modern, **$1**.

BG, small, pressed creating a
lacy-like design, brass loop
and plate shank, old, **$2**.

BG, small, flat rim with raised
center design, two-way hump
shank, old, **$1**.

BG, diminutive, self-shank, square shape, paint finish, old, **$2**.

BG, diminutive, self-shank, oval shape, imitation pearl OME, old, **$1**.

BG, diminutive, two-way
hump shank, beautiful
design, old, **$2**.

BG, small, molded with polished center and silver luster, this button is of very fine quality, **$4.**

The reverse of the molded button on the previous page has a wonderful back mark, "PAT'D DEC 28, 1880." Note that the shank, while still a metal loop and shank, is set into the glass, unlike others in this section. Buttons such as these are called "1880s." The back mark refers to a patent for an improved method of inserting the shank into the glass, by a New York button maker. That's right...this button is American made.

BG, small, self-shank, square with white pearlescent center and gold luster, modern, **$2**.

BG, small, self-shank, center is raised, heavily "carved" border with gold luster, modern, **$2**.

BG, small, self-shank,
gold luster, modern, **$1**
each.

BG, small, self-shank, Hobnail design with gold luster, modern, **$1**.

BG, small, self-shank, both gold luster on border and silver luster in center, modern, **$1**.

BG, small, self-shank, gold luster, modern, **$1**.

BG, small, self-shank, incised rose design, modern, **$1**.

BG, medium, metal shank set in formed glass extension, dome shape with Art Nouveau-style flowers, silver luster over all. This is a gorgeous older button, probably 1890, **$5**.

BG, medium, molded with incised flowers, silver luster, back marked with single star, modern, self-shank, **$2**.

BG, medium, lion design, self-shank, silver luster, new, **$2**, due to pictorial design.

BG, medium, four-leaf clover design, silver luster, self-shank, modern, **$3**.

Two BG, small, self-
shanks, silver luster,
modern, **$1** each.

BG, small, self-shank, silver luster, modern, **$1**.

BG, small, four-way box shank, silver luster, old, **$4**.

BG, small, self-shank, impressed floral design with silver luster, modern, **$1**.

BG, small, self-shank, raised leaf and border design with silver luster, modern, **$2**.

BG, small, silver luster, old, **$4**. Shank is a four-way box with sewing grooves and metal plate and loop. Beautifully crafted perhaps in the design of an owl?

BG, small, silver luster, old, **$3**. Shank is a four-way box with sewing grooves and metal plate and loop. Beautifully crafted in the design of a star.

Both buttons are BG, small, silver luster, old, **$3** each. Shanks are four-way box with sewing grooves and metal plate and loop. Beautifully crafted in the designs of an Art Nouveau-style flower and bowl of berries.

BG, small, metal plate and loop shank, old, chipped in several places on the back and side, as is, **$4**; in excellent condition it could be worth **$10**. Bet you thought it was a metal button... I did. The center has a red luster applied, while the pieces in relief (bee and flowers) have a silver luster.

BG, small, self-shank, silver luster with rhinestone, or "paste," OME, new, **$2**.

BG set in plastic, large, brass loop and plate shank, pressed glass center has gold luster, modern, **$3**. This is an example of how glass can be set in other materials.

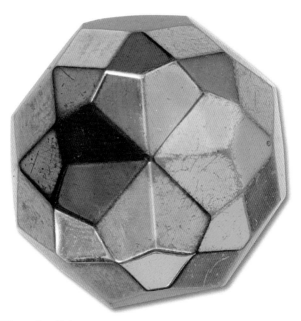

BG, small, self-shank, modern, **$2**. Several luster colors have been applied to this faceted button, giving it the star affect you see.

BG, small, self-shank, luster appears silver, but, on closer inspection, is blue, modern, **$1**.

BG, small, small brass loop and plate shank, old, **$3**. This pressed button has a faceted center and an aurora luster was applied to the center only, giving the button a flower appearance.

BG, small, self-shank, copper luster, modern, **$3**. While not rare, this color is harder to find.

BG, small (barely), self-shank, white paint in center, outer glass is faceted, early modern, **$1**.

BG, small, self-shank, matte finish on glass with impressed painted floral design, modern, **$2.**

BG, medium, self-shank, faceted and recessed circular sections with paint, modern, **$2** (with good paint).

Clear and colored glass

The buttons in this section follow the same guidelines as black glass buttons and all of them, unless otherwise noted, have molded designs with self-shanks, are modern, and of West German origin.

Aurora or aurora borealis glass is glass with a beautiful luster that came out of West Germany from 1957 to 1963.

Moonglows are buttons that are constructed with a thin layer of clear glass over the color layer. It can cover all or a portion of the button. They were manufactured in West Germany from the mid-1950s until the early 1960s.

Light blue glass, small, "Kiddie Button" picturing a water bird (heron?), **$1.50**.

Royal blue glass, small, "Le Chic" (B. Blumenthal Co. USA importers/distributors), back mark, **$2**.

Light blue glass, small, gold luster on toy train that travels around the button, **$1.50**.

Blue glass, very small, square shape with paint DF, **$2**.

Royal blue glass, small, square shape with gold luster on border, Moonglow, **$2**.

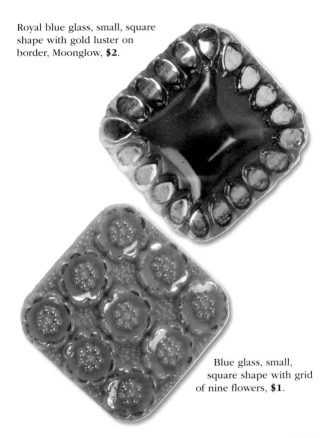

Blue glass, small, square shape with grid of nine flowers, **$1**.

Blue glass, small, pierced design (not easy to find), with gold luster, **$4**.

Blue glass, medium, aurora luster, **$2**.

Navy blue glass, small, gold luster, **$1**.

Blue glass, very small, flower center, gold luster and green paint, has wonderful detail for such a small button, **$2**.

Blue glass, small, sew-through (not very common), gold luster, **$1**.

Blue glass, small, realistic mouse, Moonglow with black paint, New Czech, **$3**.

Red glass, small,
realistic ladybug
with black and
white paint, **$1.50**.

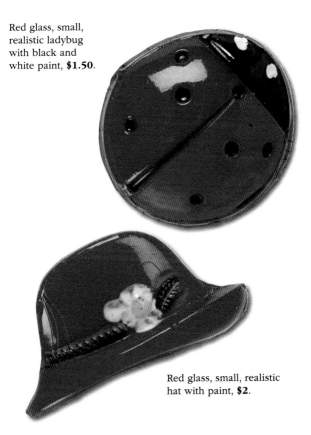

Red glass, small, realistic
hat with paint, **$2**.

Red glass, small, Art Deco design, **$1.50**.

Red glass, small, gold luster, back marked "LeChic," **$2**.

Glass, medium, silver luster, $4. This is a new Czech button that imitates the design of lacy glass made in the early 1900s. It is unclear if this button is clear glass with a layer of green underneath (as with true lacy glass) or green glass. The silver backing is typical of some of the new Czech buttons, while lacys had a black painted backing.

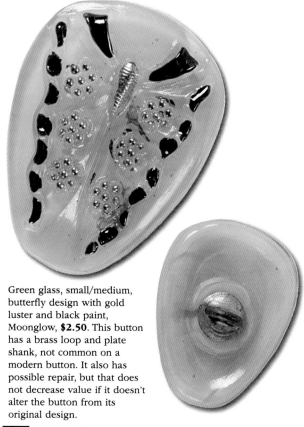

Green glass, small/medium, butterfly design with gold luster and black paint, Moonglow, **$2.50**. This button has a brass loop and plate shank, not common on a modern button. It also has possible repair, but that does not decrease value if it doesn't alter the button from its original design.

Green glass, large, imitation fabric design (basket weave), satin finish (another modern West German creation), 1960s, four-way box shank, **$3**.

Green glass, small, cute duck design with painted background, **$3**.

White glass, medium, pictorial dog button with paint DF, **$3**.

White glass, small, realistic cauliflower design, paint DF, one of a set of eight vegetables made in glass and plastic, **$4**.

White glass, small, molded anchor design, paint DF, **$1**.

White glass, medium, etched design with blue DF, **$2**.

Pink glass, small, Moonglow, **$2**.

Pink glass, small, aurora DF, **$1**.

Pink glass, medium, molded top, overall flower design with
aurora DF, **$2**.

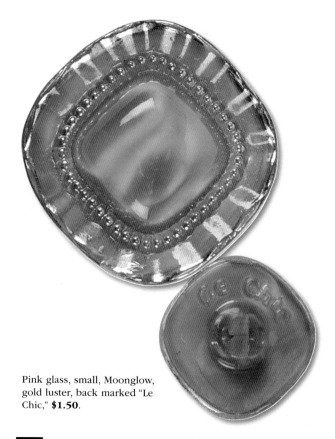

Pink glass, small, Moonglow, gold luster, back marked "Le Chic," **$1.50**.

Gold/yellow glass, small, typical geometric shape with aurora DF, **$1.50**.

Orange glass, small, swirled design with aurora DF, **$1.50**.

Caramel glass, medium,
molded shell design with
metallic pink luster, **$1.50**.

Caramel glass, small, lovely
Art Deco design with gold
luster, DF, **$2**.

Yellow glass, small,
realistic jingle bell design,
self-shank, **$1**.

Amber glass, small, translucent, heart within a heart, **$2**.

Gray glass, very small, Moonglow with silver luster border, **$1**.

Brown glass,
very small, silver
luster, **$1**.

Clear glass, small,
molded flower, painted
back, gold luster center
top, New Czech glass, **$3**.

Clear glass, small, molded
berry design, painted back,
$1.

Clear glass, small, fluted border surrounds a large rhinestone (talk about bling!), aurora DF, **$2**.

Clear glass, medium, molded berry design, back has painted "mercury" finish, sometimes inaccurately called "mirror back," **$1.50**.

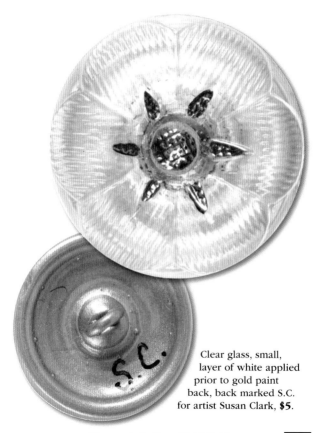

Clear glass, small,
layer of white applied
prior to gold paint
back, back marked S.C.
for artist Susan Clark, **$5**.

Paperweight

Paperweight buttons were first made in 1941 exclusively for collectors by glass artisans. Fortunately their art is well documented and each artist has their own recognizable style. The finer the quality, the higher price they command. They are very fragile.

Paperweight button, small. Artist Thura Erickson made this type of flower paperweight button from 1945-1960. This type of button by this artist can cost **$75+**.

Intermixed and striped or candy-striped glass

One of my favorite types of glass is striped glass. The following are pictures of this type of glass buttons that look good enough to eat!

The gray button, bottom right, is actually a DUG (Design Under Glass) made by Schwanda in West Germany in the 1940s. Center button is a Moonglow; silver and gold luster DFs, **$1-$3** each.

Clear, white and amber glass stripes, top right back marked "Costumakers," **50 cents-$1** each.

Candy stripes and blue intermixed flower, **$1** each.

Striped glass in lovely designs, **$1-$2** each.

Two beautiful striped glass Moonglows with gold luster, **$2** each.

Metals

Entire books have been written discussing single types of metal buttons, so I will not pretend that I can do justice to the subject in this small space. Regardless, metal buttons are, in my opinion, some of the most varied and beautiful buttons ever made. I hope that you will do more research if you spot something that piques your interest.

Metals can be discussed in several categories, two of which I will touch on in this chapter: material and construction.

Button materials shown here include silver, pewter, steel, aluminum, brass, and copper. Miscellaneous metals are referred to as white and yellow metals. All of these button types are easy to find. Metal buttons in mint condition, however, are not so easily found. Moisture and oils from our hands can quickly cause metals to deteriorate, so it is important to keep these buttons dry and handle them with a dry cloth (especially steel).

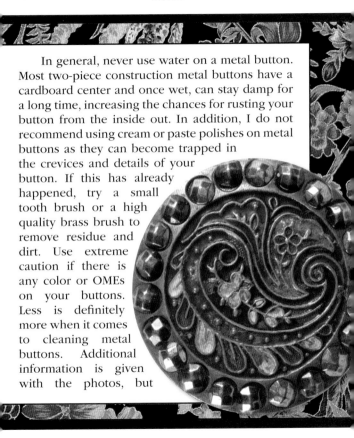

In general, never use water on a metal button. Most two-piece construction metal buttons have a cardboard center and once wet, can stay damp for a long time, increasing the chances for rusting your button from the inside out. In addition, I do not recommend using cream or paste polishes on metal buttons as they can become trapped in the crevices and details of your button. If this has already happened, try a small tooth brush or a high quality brass brush to remove residue and dirt. Use extreme caution if there is any color or OMEs on your buttons. Less is definitely more when it comes to cleaning metal buttons. Additional information is given with the photos, but

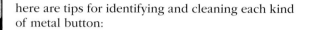

here are tips for identifying and cleaning each kind of metal button:

Aluminum

These buttons are easily identified by their white color and lightness of weight. Recently aluminum was used to make small, painted novelty buttons (back marked JHB), but it has never been a popular material for button making. A polishing cloth is great for cleaning.

Brass

Brass is a common material for buttons. It has the color and luster of gold, without the weight or cost. Brass is also more malleable than copper or zinc, making it a good choice for casting. Because it is an alloy (copper and zinc) it can be made softer or harder by varying its composition. A good quality brass brush (see resources) works well for removing the green powder that often infects these buttons, as well as cleaning dirt from any grooves. Vinegar, on a cotton swab, can also be used if you

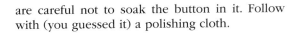

are careful not to soak the button in it. Follow with (you guessed it) a polishing cloth.

Copper

Copper is easily identified by its color. A polishing cloth should be used for cleaning.

Pewter

Pewter buttons contain lead, so if you rub the side of the button on white paper, it will leave a "pencil" mark. A polishing cloth works well for cleaning, but here is a unique method you can also use: buff your pewter button with the outer leaf from a cabbage head. Follow up with a soft, dry cloth.

Silver

Most silver buttons fall into two categories: Mexican and Indian silver, and hallmarked silver. Mexican and Indian silver can often be identified by their design and shank styles. Hallmarked silver

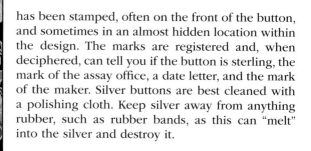

has been stamped, often on the front of the button, and sometimes in an almost hidden location within the design. The marks are registered and, when deciphered, can tell you if the button is sterling, the mark of the assay office, a date letter, and the mark of the maker. Silver buttons are best cleaned with a polishing cloth. Keep silver away from anything rubber, such as rubber bands, as this can "melt" into the silver and destroy it.

Steel

A magnet will identify a steel button. Remember that buttons can be made of a mixture of metals, so you may have a steel embellishment, but not a steel button. Handle steel buttons as little as possible. I like to use the small cloths you can get to clean your eye glasses with to handle these buttons. A polishing cloth will clean your steel buttons. Rust can be removed with an ink eraser, but it may return. A chemical rust remover such as WD-40 or Naval Jelly can be applied with a cotton swab. Leave it on overnight and remove with a clean, dry swab. Follow with the polishing cloth.

Metal construction types include some of the most beautiful details found on buttons:

Faceted steels

These are tiny bits of steel that have been cut and polished to resemble diamonds. They would be attached to the button by riveting each piece to a ring or base. Imitation "steels" were also made by punching the design from the underside of a single metal piece. Steels can be used as a single OME on a button, or cover the entire surface of the button.

Steel ring, front and back. Note the rivets and brass base on the back view.

Steel cups

The base of the button is cup shaped, to varying degrees, and the edge continues to the front of the button to form a rim. The center of the button that is held in the "cup" does not have to be steel, or even metal, as you will see. The rim is often beautifully formed and the centers can have exquisite detail.

Twinkles

Twinkle buttons can be simple or elaborate, and the twinkle portion can be a single tiny element confined to the border or cover the entire surface of the button. These two-piece buttons are defined by a pierced top through which a reflective surface, or liner, can be seen. Liners come in a variety of colors. This is a fairly simplistic definition, but you will understand when you see them.

This is a short list, but you will discover other fabulous button types as you peruse the metal buttons in this chapter.

Brass, small, constructed of stamped brass characters applied to a textured brass cup, with a flat white metal crescent moon attached under the rim, **$5**. This is a common button titled "True Love" and depicts French pantomime characters Pierrot and Pierrette. It was made in several sizes as well as in black glass.

Brass, small, two-piece construction with tunnel-style shank, early 1900s, **$8**. Teddy bear buttons of this style became popular after the infamous Theodore Roosevelt incident.

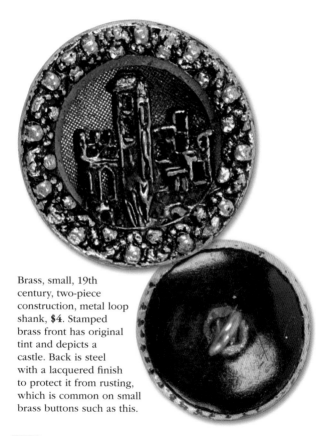

Brass, small, 19th
century, two-piece
construction, metal loop
shank, **$4**. Stamped
brass front has original
tint and depicts a
castle. Back is steel
with a lacquered finish
to protect it from rusting,
which is common on small
brass buttons such as this.

Brass, small (7/16"),
two-piece construction,
has a similar construction
to previous button, **$2**.

Brass, small, two-piece construction, stamped, tinted and pierced brass with velvet lining. Back is a tunnel-style shank, **$2**. This type of button is called a "perfume" button, as ladies dabbed perfume on the buttons to scent themselves.

Brass, small, two-piece construction, stamped applied leaf design with white metal "collet" under the rim, **$1**.

Brass, medium, one piece, stamped and enameled design, surrounded by cut steels, brass loop shank. Believe it or not, this is one of a set of eight I found in a bag full of button treasures at a thrift store. The whole bag cost me $4; this button alone is valued at **$25**!

Brass, medium, two-piece construction, front is one piece, molded and stamped, back is steel with tunnel-style shank, **$1**.

Brass, large (1-1/2"), two-piece construction, steel back with U-shaped shank, top has a slight peak with stamped design, **$2**. Another thrift store find, six of these were on a sweater!

Brass, small, two-piece construction, carved pearl center, **$1**.

Copper, small (3/4"), two-hole sew-through, new, **$1.50**.

Copper, medium, loop shank, punched design, 1960s, **$10**. Cards of copper buttons with Native American design work were made and sold to tourists in the South West when travel along Route 66 beckoned Americans to see more of their country.

Pewter, small, "bright cut" construction, metal loop shank, **$7**. Bright cut pewters are dyed and then stamped and cut using a sharp tool. This one also has a faceted steel OME.

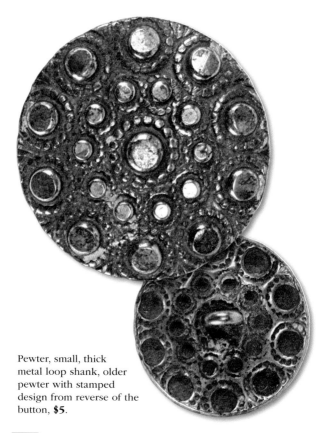

Pewter, small, thick
metal loop shank, older
pewter with stamped
design from reverse of the
button, **$5**.

Pewter, small, pewter
shank soldered on
separately, cast and
carved design base with
yellow metal OME, **$2**.

Pewter, small, large metal
loop shank, heart design
is pierced through,
new button from B.
Blumenthal Co.,
$1.

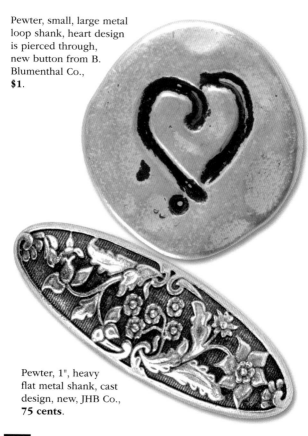

Pewter, 1", heavy
flat metal shank, cast
design, new, JHB Co.,
75 cents.

Pewter, 1-1/4", applied metal shank, hand-cast with design, front and back, made by Danforth Pewters, **$8**.

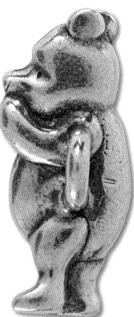

Pewter, large, heavy metal shank, center OME is synthetic imitation dyed shell, new from JHB Co., **$3**.

Pewter, medium, metal shank, pierced design, new, JHB Co., **$3**.

Silver, medium, Native
American, punched
design set with turquoise,
copper loop shank, **$30-$50**.

Silver, medium, Mexican, punched design, copper pin shank, **$15**.

Silver, medium, English,
hallmarked, narrow, flat
shank, cast design, **$50+**.

Steel, small, "flat steel" construction type, metal loop shank, brass dog head OME, the steel base piece must be perfectly flat to be considered for this construction type, **$6**.

Steel, small, base appears to be flat but, in fact, has a slight curve to it, cut border, center flower is punched steel and connected to the metal loop shank, forming a type of pin shank, **$2**.

Steel, small, blued
steel cup construction,
rim is plain, metal
plate with shank
connected to the white
metal center, **$6**.

Steel, small, steel cup with embossed rim, carved pearl center, pin shank, **$7**.

Steel, small, steel cup with beautifully detailed rim, omega-shaped metal shank, center has three exquisitely formed flowers set with three side and one center steels, **$7**. Has amazing detail for such a small button!

Steel, small, cut and riveted steel, a popular button construction style of the late 19th century, loop shank, **$5**. Note how each steel is individually attached.

Steel, small, from the front, this appears to be a blued steel cup, but a look at it shows the two-piece construction (with metal loop shank), center has nine blued steels, lovely button, **$10**.

White metal, small, two-piece construction, stamped design, back is steel with tunnel-style shank, **$1**.

White metal, small, domed top with beautifully detailed stamped design, flat metal shank, **$2**.

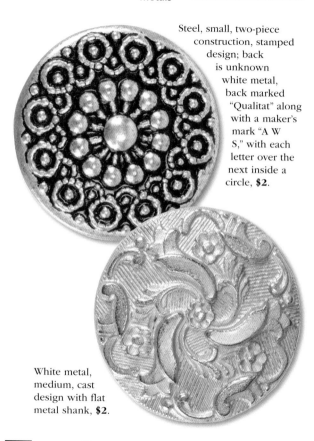

Steel, small, two-piece construction, stamped design; back is unknown white metal, back marked "Qualitat" along with a maker's mark "A W S," with each letter over the next inside a circle, **$2**.

White metal, medium, cast design with flat metal shank, **$2**.

White metal, medium, pierced design set with rhinestones, newer button, **$2**.

Yellow metal, medium, one-piece cast and pierced design, button is a reproduction (and therefore new), but still lovely, even imitating cut steels, **$3**.

Metal twinkles

A mother/daughter pair of twinkles. The larger is 7/8" and the smaller only 7/16". The back of the larger button is back marked "Tchecoslovaquie" with three stars beneath it and the spelling indicates this button was manufactured during the WWI era, **$2/$1**.

Another mother/daughter pair, these have a twinkle border. The larger button is 1-1/2" and the smaller is 3/4". This rose is a fairly common design, **$3/$1**.

Sew-through twinkle buttons are not common, but this particular design is a common one, **$1**.

Twinkles come in
wonderful shapes and
this square button has
a convex-shaped top
and is almost pillow
shaped, small, **$2**.

A modified ball shape, small, **$2**.

Twinkles also come in a variety of sizes. The button at the top is diminutive in size; the middle button is also diminutive, as well as ball shaped; the bottom button is very small. All three shine just as nicely as a larger twinkle button, **$1** each.

Brass, small, twinkle, steel back with back mark "Geschutzt" and "Gesetzl" with a star between each word, **$2**.

Two lovely, older
twinkle buttons,
medium size, **$1**
each.

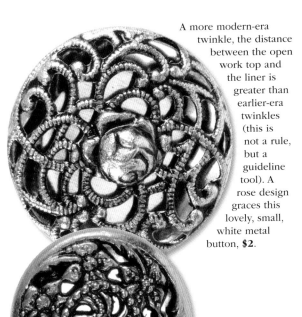

A more modern-era twinkle, the distance between the open work top and the liner is greater than earlier-era twinkles (this is not a rule, but a guideline tool). A rose design graces this lovely, small, white metal button, **$2**.

White metal, small, twinkle, lovely detail, **$1**.

Brass, medium, twinkle, grapes and leaves on the vine form the
open work, **$1**.

While this button may look like a twinkle button, it is not. The liner is made from celluloid and is transparent, rather than reflective. Still, it is a lovely button, **$1**.

This button does have a reflective ring around the rim, but this is not considered a liner, rather it is called a collet, **$2**.

Plastics

In this day and age it's difficult, if not impossible, to think of our lives without plastics. They can be molded to any shape we can imagine and the products are durable. Making buttons and other products was now fast and cheap. While this sounds like a wonderful advancement, it actually put an end to finely crafted buttons that had been available in the past. Craftsmen couldn't compete with mass production and the result of this is what we think of as the common button: small, round, four-hole shirt buttons.

Plastic is a complex subject. It is a word that covers a wide variety of chemical, as well as natural, substances. While I enjoyed chemistry in school, my lesson here is about buttons, so I will use the word in a general way. In this chapter I will, briefly, discuss four types of common types of plastics used to make buttons: celluloid, Bakelite, composition, and modern plastics.

Celluloid

Celluloid is considered to be the first plastic-like substance. It was discovered by a British chemist, Alexander Parkes, in 1869, and first used in the manufacturing process by American John Wesley Hyatt in the early 1870s. Celluloid is made from a mix of nitrocellulose and camphor. This mix produces several results when it comes to buttons. Cellulose is the fibrous cell wall of plants and as with any natural material it will decay. When this happens, the other chemicals in the mix are released, and can damage your other buttons. Another property of celluloid is that it is flammable.

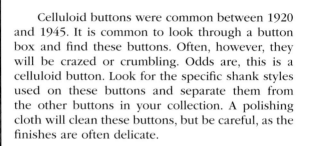

Celluloid buttons were common between 1920 and 1945. It is common to look through a button box and find these buttons. Often, however, they will be crazed or crumbling. Odds are, this is a celluloid button. Look for the specific shank styles used on these buttons and separate them from the other buttons in your collection. A polishing cloth will clean these buttons, but be careful, as the finishes are often delicate.

Bakelite

Bakelite is the first true, all-chemical plastic. It is named for its Belgian inventor, Leo Baekeland (1909). Bakelite items, including buttons, are very collectible, and therefore command higher prices. The shapes and colors of Bakelite buttons are distinct, though Bakelite does fade with time. A couple of tests will help you identify Bakelite. Try rubbing the piece with your finger until it is warm. There should be an unmistakable smell of formaldehyde. You can also use a cleaning product called "Scrubbing Bubbles." Wet the end of a cotton swab with the product and wipe the back of the button with the swab. The swab will turn yellow (and the button will be unharmed) if the button is made from Bakelite. Clean them carefully, as Bakelite has a very thin layer of "finish" on it. You can use a damp cloth, such as a diaper or old T-shirt. A gentle dish soap can be used if needed. I have read of other methods, but I have not personally used them. As always, I recommend the least harsh method possible.

Composition

Composition buttons are not always easy to identify. The term is used to describe any button made from a binder, such as shellac, and a filler, including mica, giving some of these buttons a faint sparkle. One type of composition button is termed "fleck," because the fillers include various colors and bits of tinsel and pearl chips that give the button its design element. Black composition buttons are often mistaken for rubber buttons. These can be cleaned with a damp cloth or a polishing cloth.

Modern plastics

Modern plastics were developed in the 1920s. Collectable buttons from this early era in plastics history include Art Deco-style buttons (1930-1945), and "goofie" buttons (1930-1949). "Goofies" are realistically shaped buttons that mimic the shape of a real object. I find it especially fun to study them because they imitate objects commonly found during that time period. For example, buttons shaped like fruit became popular after Carmen Miranda wore her infamous hat made from fruit. Many "goofies" were made in sets and are especially nice to collect.

Plastic buttons are a great and inexpensive place to start collecting buttons. They may not have the same value as buttons made from other materials, but they are certainly fun, colorful, and plentiful. Many plastic buttons can be used without fear of damage on wonderful sewing and craft projects. I have always felt it important to enjoy your collection by using your buttons whenever possible.

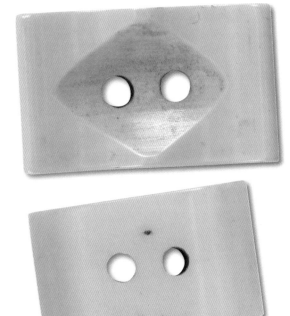

Bakelite, small, two-hole sew-through, typical color of
natural Bakelite (aged), **$2**.

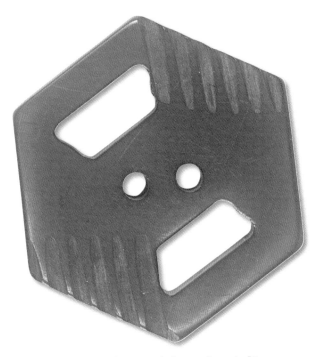

Bakelite, medium, two-hole sew-through, **$2**.

Bakelite, large, inserted metal loop shank, 1930s ladies coat button, metal OME, these large and ornate buttons are very collectible, **$15-$25** typically.

Bakelite, 2" long, tunnel shank; another typical shape, this rod-style button came in many wonderful colors and sizes, **$3**.

Bakelite "cookie" buttons, two-hole sew-through, called
cookies because they look like they were sliced from a
roll of refrigerated cookie dough, identical front and back;
small is **$2**; medium is **$5**.

Bakelite, realistic monkey, two-hole sew-through, many realistic buttons were made like this and this is too fun, **$18**.

Bakelite, large,
typical Bakelite color
and design, **$5**.

Celluloid, large, applied plastic shank, "knot" or "rods and strands"-style button, made from extruded strands of celluloid, **$5**.

Celluloid, large
(1-1/4"), metal loop
shank, celluloid
background with
stamped metal trims,
typical late 19th century, **$20**.

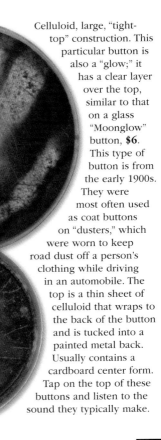

Celluloid, large, "tight-top" construction. This particular button is also a "glow;" it has a clear layer over the top, similar to that on a glass "Moonglow" button, **$6**. This type of button is from the early 1900s. They were most often used as coat buttons on "dusters," which were worn to keep road dust off a person's clothing while driving in an automobile. The top is a thin sheet of celluloid that wraps to the back of the button and is tucked into a painted metal back. Usually contains a cardboard center form. Tap on the top of these buttons and listen to the sound they typically make.

Celluloid, medium, "tight-top" construction, "glow" bubble top, recessed center is a metal liner, giving this button the more accentuated glow you see here, **$3**.

Celluloid, large, "tight-top" construction; an especially lovely example, the top has an offset center that appears "pinched," **$3**.

Celluloid, large, inserted metal
loop shank, solid "bar," **$3**.

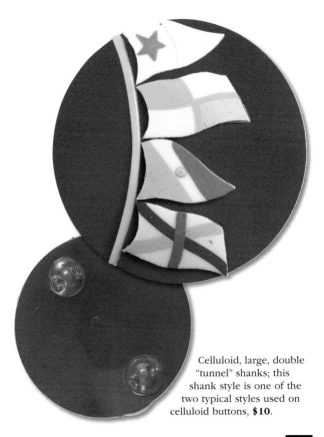

Celluloid, large, double
"tunnel" shanks; this
shank style is one of the
two typical styles used on
celluloid buttons, **$10**.

Celluloid, large, construction of this button is, for lack of a better term, a "reverse tight-top;" the front of the button has a raised rim as well as a raised center, the purple back comes over to the front to hold the front piece, typical tunnel shank, **$3**.

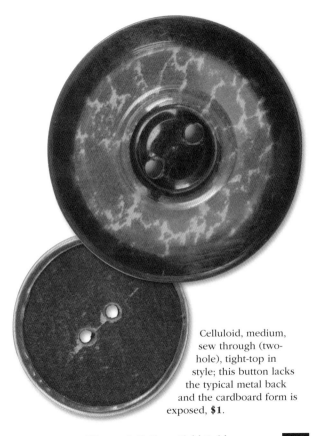

Celluloid, medium, sew through (two-hole), tight-top in style; this button lacks the typical metal back and the cardboard form is exposed, **$1**.

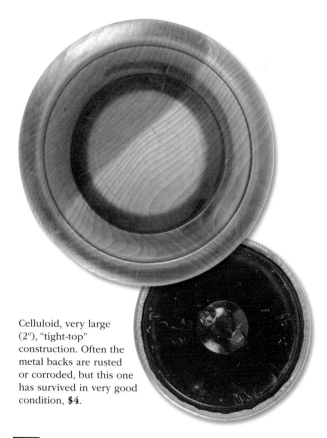

Celluloid, very large (2"), "tight-top" construction. Often the metal backs are rusted or corroded, but this one has survived in very good condition, $4.

Celluloid, medium, tunnel shank, molded raised top, navy blue with painted flowers in center. If you look carefully at the edge of this button, you can see where the top was joined to the back, **$2**.

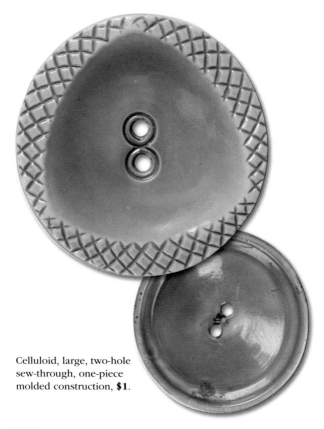

Celluloid, large, two-hole
sew-through, one-piece
molded construction, **$1**.

Celluloid, small, tunnel
shank, lovely molded
design, cone shape, **$2**.

Celluloid, medium,
tunnel shank, tight-top
with molded raised top,
mint condition, $3.

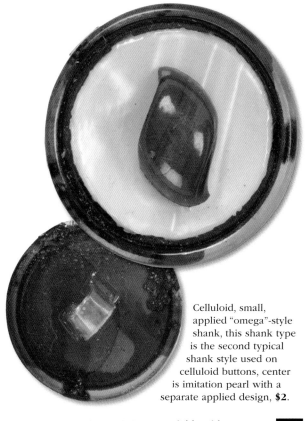

Celluloid, small, applied "omega"-style shank, this shank type is the second typical shank style used on celluloid buttons, center is imitation pearl with a separate applied design, **$2**.

Celluloid, small (1/2"),
applied "omega"-style
shank, carved design, **$1**.

Celluloid, small, tunnel shank, **$1**.

Celluloid, medium,
tunnel shank, domed
top with great, but typical
style design, **$2**.

Celluloid, medium,
applied "omega" shank,
has a fun, molded flower
design, **$1**.

Celluloid, medium, tunnel shank, **$1**.

Celluloid, medium, tight-
top with tunnel shank,
top resembles carved
wood, **$1**.

Celluloid overlay buttons, all are medium, typical two-hole sew-through. A thin layer of celluloid is applied over the thicker base of another color and the design is carved into the top, revealing the bottom color layer. This green color is typical for the top layer, with creme or black for the base, **50 cents** each.

These are also medium-sized celluloid overlay buttons with the typical two-hole sew-through. They resemble poker chips; **50 cents** each.

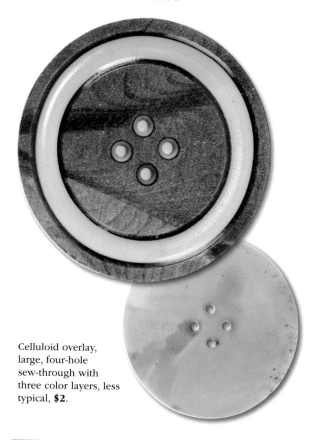

Celluloid overlay,
large, four-hole
sew-through with
three color layers, less
typical, **$2**.

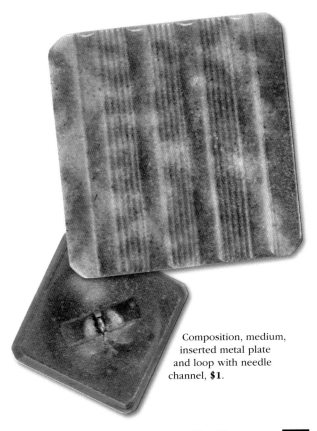

Composition, medium, inserted metal plate and loop with needle channel, **$1**.

Composition, medium,
inserted metal plate
and loop with needle
channel, **$1**.

Composition, very large
(1-1/2"), self-shank with
needle channel, **$3**.

Composition, medium,
self-shank with needle
channel, **$1**.

Composition, medium,
self-shank with needle
channel, **$1**.

Composition, medium, self-shank with needle channel, **$1**.

Fleck composition, whistle construction, **$1**.

Plastic, large, knob-style
self-shank with needle
channel, lovely design, **$2**.

Plastic, very large
(1-1/2") and large knob-
style self-shank with
needle channel, another
lovely design, **$3**.

Plastic, very large
(1-1/2") and large knob-
style self-shank with
needle channel, **$3**.

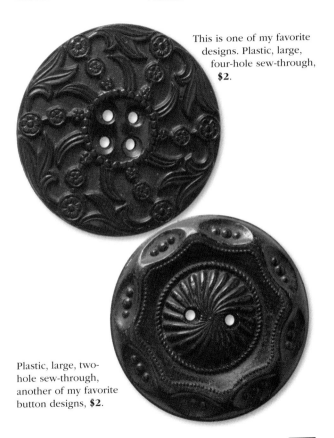

This is one of my favorite designs. Plastic, large, four-hole sew-through, **$2**.

Plastic, large, two-hole sew-through, another of my favorite button designs, **$2**.

Plastic, possibly acrylic, very large, metal back with loop shank, **$15**. This is a fascinating button! The plastic rim holds a clear, domed top and a design is etched and painted in the center of the transparent cover, as well as the liner seen through the top. It is either an exquisite newer button or a remarkably well preserved older button. The jury is still out, despite my best attempts to identify it. Just ask yourself: does it really matter? Not at all.

Plastic, small, molded
shank, has an
"embedded" design,
where pieces of foil are
molded in the plastic,
50 cents.

Plastic, medium, self-shank, new, etched and painted to resemble wood, **75 cents**.

Plastic whistle buttons in various sizes, same design, **50 cents** each.

Plastic, medium, whistle in
imitation tortoise shell, **$1**.

Plastic, small, whistle,
pink rose design, **$1**.

Plastic, medium, applied plastic shank, transfer design of Winnie the Pooh onto clear plastic, one of a set of characters from A.A. Milne books, new, **$2**.

Plastic, small, two-hole sew-through, this new button imitates children's bone underwear buttons and many were painted with cute faces such as this, **$1**.

Polymer clay, medium, two-hole sew-through, new, three-dimensional, realistic teddy bear distributed by B. Blumenthal Co.; made by rolling clay and attaching the pieces together, the piece is then baked to set the design, **$2**.

Polymer clay, mediums, two-hole sew-throughs, these
beautifully hand-crafted buttons are flat. A tube of clay is made
by carefully layering colors, shaping the tube, and slicing
the buttons off like cookies and baked, **$2-$4**. Created and
distributed by Just Another Button Company.

Plastic, smalls, molded plastic shanks, rocking horse design, with and without a rider, typical 1930s realistic buttons, **$1** each.

Plastics, small to medium, plastic self-shanks, various lion designs, the green button being the oldest and the larger, gold lion being the newest, **$1** each.

Plastics, small to medium, self-shanks, new. Paddington Bear button is back marked "EDEN 92"; both were distributed by JHB Co., **75 cents** each.

Plastic, medium, self-shank, design depicts leaves and berries. This design can be found in many different materials. Some people (like me) enjoy collecting one design in as many materials and colors as possible, **$1**.

This group of plastic buttons are called "kiddie" buttons. While these are newer buttons, kiddie buttons were made from glass and plastic for use on children's clothing in the 1930s, **50 cents** each.

Plastic, small, self-shank, new, realistic button-shaped like an ear of corn. This is a "snap together" button; the yellow corn, which has the shank on the back of it, will come apart from the green leaves if you push on the shank, **50 cents**.

Plastic, small, self-shank, 1930s, realistic "goofie" in the shape of a crown, **$1**.

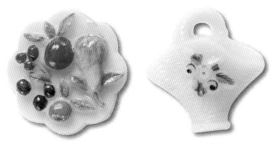

Plastics, small, early 1900s, self-shanks, realistic fruit plate and basket, also called "goofies," part of a set, **$1** each.

Plastics, smalls, self-shanks, 1930s realistic "goofies." Who can resist these fun buttons? **$1** each.

Plastic, medium, two-hole
sew-through, 1930s, a
great design, **$2**.

The buttons here and through Page 317 are typical, colorful, plentiful, and fun! Made in the 1930s and 1940s, they came in various colors with the same design. Most have a typical "hollow" back. Collecting these is like hoarding candy! Most can be found for **25 cents** each.

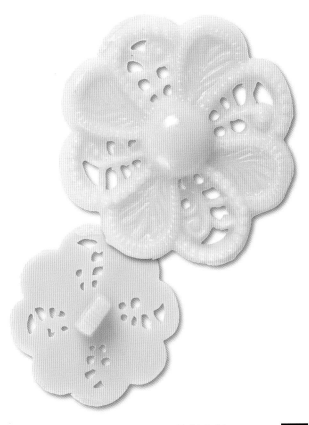

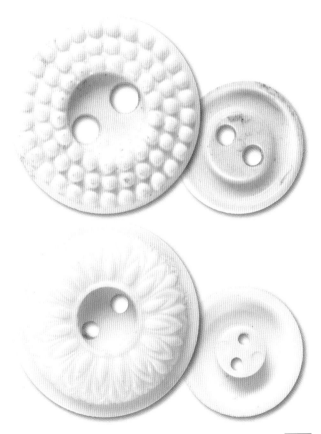

These buttons are the pride of the JHB line. In 1976, the company acquired the exclusive licensing rights to the Beatrix Potter characters, and produced several series sets depicting the sweet characters from Ms. Potter's books. Mrs. Jean Howard Barr, founder and CEO of JHB, is proud of the line and enjoys collecting related items. I was recently privileged to see Mrs. Barr's collection of Beatrix Potter books, printed in several languages. In addition, I am pleased to say that Mrs. Barr is an active member in the Colorado State Button Society. She is a very gracious and delightful lady and we are all grateful for her contributions to the button industry and button collecting.

Most are still available as new buttons at retail prices; discontinued ones would bring higher prices.

Rubber

Rubber buttons are, in my opinion, one of the most rewarding types of buttons to find. They are so plain that they are very often overlooked in a box of old buttons. They are most often black, but other colors were made as well. Flip them over and you will know, instantly, that you have found a rubber button because they are always back marked.

When Charles Goodyear patented his process for making vulcanized rubber in 1844, his brother, Nelson, decided to make a few products of his own using this new technology. In 1849, Nelson took out a patent for "elastic cords for suspenders," and then in 1851 he received a patent for a hard rubber substance that he used to make durable buttons.

Goodyear's rubber buttons were manufactured only in the US. The most common back mark found on rubber buttons is "Goodyear's patent" and the date 1851 along with the manufacturer's name. Dates are commonly found and include, in some form, 1849-1851. After Goodyear's patent expired, other companies made these buttons as well. Manufacturers' initials include:

N.R.Co.—Novelty Rubber Company (New York and New Jersey).

I.R.C.Co.—India Rubber Comb Company (New York).

D.H.R.Co.—Dickinson Hard Rubber Company (Massachusetts). This also includes the date 1875, which is probably the date that the company was incorporated.

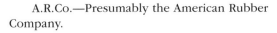

A.R.Co.—Presumably the American Rubber Company.

AHR Co.—American Hard Rubber Company.

P=T—patent.

Rubber buttons can be cleaned with a soft brush and polishing cloth. A dab of baby oil on a clean cloth can restore the luster to your button. Be sure to dry thoroughly.

The buttons in this chapter were chosen to show some of the more common patterns and construction styles that rubber buttons were made in. Back marks are listed, but others can be found. Colors are given, but they may have faded. Check near the shank to best determine color.

There is more information available about these interesting buttons that cannot be covered here. I hope you will take the time to do more reading about this subject. Happy hunting.

Black rubber, medium,
four-hole sew-through,
back mark: "I.R.C.Co.
Goodyear 1851," **$2**.

Black rubber, Navy pea coat button, large, four-hole sew-through, back mark: "AHR Co. HP," manufactured in the late 1800s, **$5**.

Dark brown rubber, medium, self-shank with guides; front: fabric pattern; back mark: "I.R.C.Co. 1851 Goodyear," early 1900s, **$2**.

Dark brown rubber, very small, pin shank, back mark: "NRCo Goodyear's P=T," **$2**.

Brown rubber, small, metal loop shank, back mark: "N.R.Co. Goodyear's P=T. 1851," **$2**.

Dark brown rubber, medium, metal loop shank; front: female head with beaded border. Back mark: "N.R.Co. Goodyear's P=T. 1851," **$5**. While this is not an uncommon button, pictorials do command higher prices.

Dark brown rubber, small, brass loop shank; front: liberty head (different from female head); back mark: "N.R.Co. Goodyear's P=T. 1851," **$5**.

Dark brown rubber, 5/8" square, brass loop shank; front: swallow; back mark: "N.R.Co. Goodyear's P=T.," **$5**.

Black rubber, small, brass loop shank; front: cone shape with concentric rings over all; back mark: "N.R.Co. Goodyear's P=T," **$3**.

Dark brown rubber, small, brass loop shank; front: doe jumping through circle; back mark: "N.R.Co. Goodyear's P=T," **$3**.

Dark brown rubber, small, brass loop shank; front: raised center, surrounded by two rows of beaded borders; back mark: "N.R.Co. Goodyear's P=T. 1851," **$5**. This button is thicker in construction, with lovely details.

Black rubber, small, brass loop shank; front: beaded cross within a beaded border; back mark: "N.R.Co. Goodyear's P=T," **$3**.

Black rubber, small, brass loop shank; front: flower; back mark: "N.R.Co. Goodyear's P=T," **$3**.

Black rubber, small, brass loop shank; front: eight-pointed star; back mark: "N.R.Co. Goodyear's P=T," **$3**.

Black rubber, small, brass loop shank; front: high cone shape, border edge and center point with smooth surface; back mark: "N.R.Co. Goodyear's P=T. 1851," **$3**.

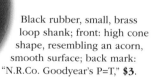

Black rubber, small, brass loop shank; front: high cone shape, resembling an acorn, smooth surface; back mark: "N.R.Co. Goodyear's P=T," **$3**.

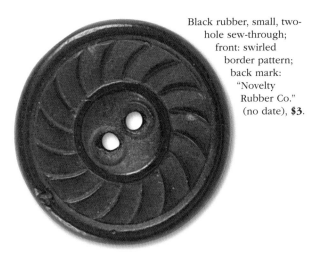

Black rubber, small, two-hole sew-through; front: swirled border pattern; back mark: "Novelty Rubber Co." (no date), **$3**.

New rubber, manufactured for Blumenthal, circa 2007, **$1.50**. This button is thin and flexible.

Shell

Chances are that you will find many shell buttons as you search through jars and boxes of buttons. Shell buttons are, for the most part, plentiful, inexpensive, and most definitely lovely.

Shell buttons can be made from many kinds of mollusks. All "pearl" buttons are shell buttons, but not all shell buttons are "pearl." The biggest differences to note are between warm water ocean shells and freshwater mussel shells. "Mother of pearl" (MOP) or simply "pearl" buttons are made from oyster shells found in the warm Pacific Ocean waters. They resemble white satin fabric with an iridescent luster that comes from the lining of the shell. American "pearl" buttons are white, but lack this iridescence. They are generally thinner and often appear to be China buttons at first glance. This type of shell was usually used for more utilitarian shirt and underwear buttons, while

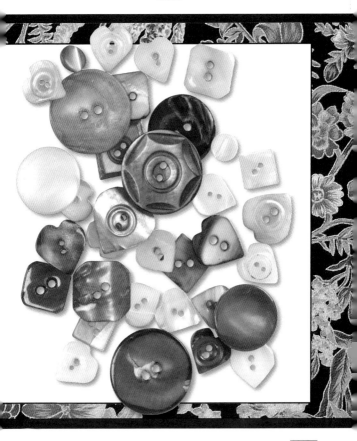

the more elegant and larger buttons were made from ocean "pearl."

Shell buttons require a good deal of labor to produce. Even the simplest shell button required a skilled person to cut the blanks as efficiently as possible and the designs were always carved by hand. Early shell buttons were imported to America chiefly from England. Around 1890, Americans began making buttons from mussel shells harvested from the Mississippi River. Soon after, abalone shells from the Baja Peninsula came into use as well.

When cleaning your shell buttons, be mindful of any paint or other embellishments that might be harmed by water or rubbing. Most shell can be gently cleaned with a soft toothbrush and mild soapy water. Baby oil on a soft cloth can help restore luster as well. Be sure to dry thoroughly.

Abalone shell, set in metal, medium, raised metal border, carved design, shell center, inserted metal shank, **$5**.

Abalone shell, small,
drilled four-way box
shank, **$1**.

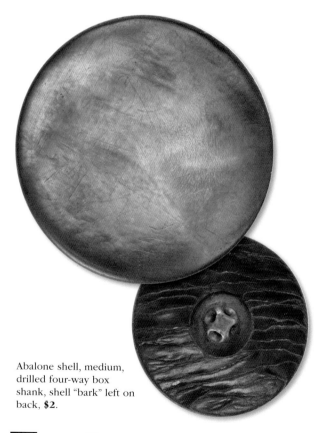

Abalone shell, medium, drilled four-way box shank, shell "bark" left on back, **$2**.

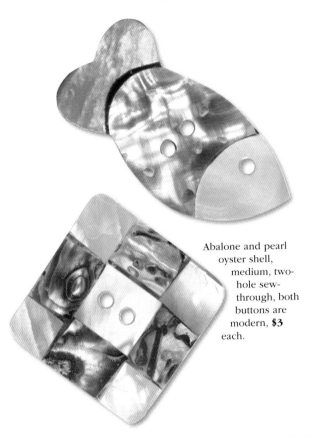

Abalone and pearl oyster shell, medium, two-hole sew-through, both buttons are modern, **$3** each.

Abalone shell, medium, two-hole sew-through, modern, **$1.50**.

Abalone shell, small, two-hole sew-through, beautiful green
color and more intricate carving, circa 1880, **$2**.

Pink abalone shell, medium, four-hole sew-through, carved swirl design, **$3.50**.

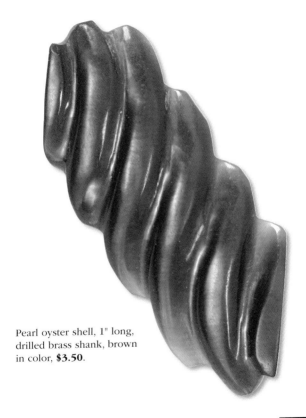

Pearl oyster shell, 1" long,
drilled brass shank, brown
in color, **$3.50**.

Pearl oyster shell, diminutive, two-hole sew-through, brown, **50 cents**.

Pearl oyster shell, medium, two-hole sew-through, pierced and carved design with delicate edge motif, 1800-1860s, **$4**.

Pearl oyster shell, medium, self-shank with drilled channel, pierced and carved design, circa 1900, **$3**.

Pearl oyster shell,
medium, pin shank,
"Colonial" style, carved,
1770-1840, **$12**.

Pearl oyster shell, medium,
drilled brass shank, carved
realistic shape (hat), circa
1800, **$3**.

Pearl oyster shell, large (1-3/4"), "Jordan" or "Bethlehem" pearl. These exquisitely carved and pierced buttons are made by artists in Bethlehem, Jordan, and the subjects depicted in the designs are Biblical in nature, **$75+**.

Pearl oyster shell, medium, four-hole sew-through, intricate carving at a variety of depths, **$1.50**.

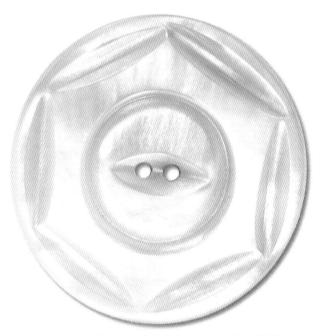

Pearl oyster shell, large, two-hole sew-through, circa 1920, common mother of pearl button, **$2**. Note the lack of intricate detail that came in the early to mid-1900s.

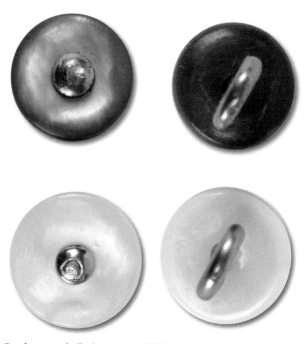

Pearl oyster shell, diminutive (3/8"), pin shank, circa 1800, **25 cents**.

Pearl oyster shell, small, pin shank with cut steel center, cut steel ring embellishment, **$5**.

Pearl oyster shell, small, pin shank with steel, star-shaped cap, lacy-style metal embellishment, **$5**.

Pearl oyster shell, medium (3/4"), pin shank, carved pearl set in flat steel base, **$3**.

Pearl oyster shell, small. This exquisite little button has two separate layers of MOP. One layer is pierced to show a metal liner beneath (a twinkle). This is then topped with a small, carved layer. These are set in a notched steel cup-shaped base. The shank is a metal loop inserted into holes that were drilled into the cup. Another metal piece is evident that appears to hold all the layers together. Very interesting construction, **$5**.

Pearl oyster shell, small, pin shank with cut steel center, "watch wheel" center, **$2**.

Pearl oyster shell, small, pin shank, but set through a half ball base made of thin metal. A steel ring, punched from the back side to resemble cut steels, borders a beautifully carved pearl center with a cut steel center, **$5**.

Pearl oyster shell, small, carved MOP center with imitation pin shank, cut steel center, twinkle screen border with blue liner, set in brass with self-shank, **$4**.

Pearl oyster shell, small, drilled metal shank, carved MOP with cut steel crescent and center OME, **$5**.

Pearl oyster shell, small, metal loop shank, a steel saucer-shaped base holds a carved pearl die set with cut steel OMEs, a fun button, **$5**.

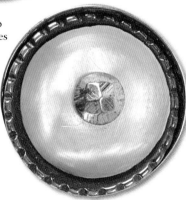

Pearl oyster shell, small, metal loop shank, carved pearl center set in pewter, **$2**. This button appears to have a pin shank, but it is fixed in position and the cut steel center is only an embellishment.

Pearl oyster shell, small, metal loop shank with drilled holes for the metal piece that holds the top pieces together, **$3**. The back is half-ball shaped and steel, and the top of the button has a separate rim set inside that "floats" and holds a smooth MOP with cut steel center. Unusual construction.

Pearl oyster shell, small, steel back with loop shank, front has a carved MOP center set in a brass twinkle border, **$4**.

Shell, medium, dyed pink, overlay, plastic base and shank, new, JHB Co., **$2.50**.

Shell, small, drilled metal shank, tin "watch wheel" center embellishment, **$3**. The pearl button was dyed red and almost looks like a glass button, but a look at the back will tell you otherwise.

Shell, small, whistle, **50 cents**.

Pearl oyster shell, medium, two-hole sew-through, circa 1900, **$1**.

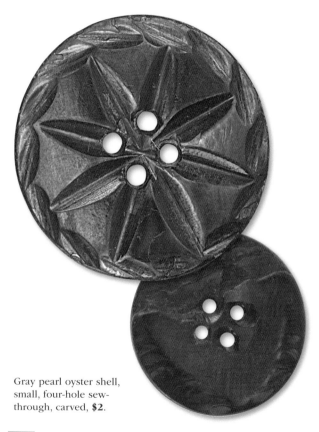

Gray pearl oyster shell,
small, four-hole sew-
through, carved, **$2**.

Gray pearl oyster shell, large, four-hole sew-through, carved center and border design, circa 1800, **$5**.

Gray pearl oyster shell, large, four-hole sew-through, carved border, **$5**.

Tiger cowry shell, small, whole shell with inserted metal shank, sold to tourists in the South Pacific, **$5**.

Tiger cowry shell, small, engraved design, **$26**.

Uniform

The arena of uniform button collecting can be a whole field to itself. Whether you collect railroad buttons, scouting buttons (as I do), or U.S. or foreign military buttons, you are in good company. These buttons are, for the most part, plentiful. Research materials are constantly being updated as information becomes available. While this is, traditionally, a man's area of collecting, many women are getting involved as well.

Most uniform buttons are back marked, which helps with dating, as well as with authenticating your button. Many buttons have been recreated for Civil War reenactments and the like. Additionally, many blazer buttons look like uniform buttons. These buttons are still collectible, but be careful of paying the price for an original button, when it is, in fact, a replica. I cannot cover all of these details here, so I encourage you to do your homework if

you decide to specialize in this area.

Most of these buttons are metal and therefore susceptible to "greening" and rust. NEVER USE WATER on metal buttons. Vinegar, applied with a swab or soft cloth can help with "the green stuff," as well as an old tooth brush. A jeweler's polishing cloth can be used to spruce them up as well, but be careful not to rub off original finishes. You want that antique button to "look" antique, don't you? When you store these buttons, keep them in a dry place, and take out any "sick" buttons, so as not to "infect" your other buttons.

Sizes are not included in this section, unless relevant.

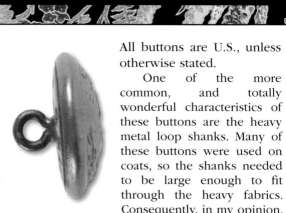

This side shank shows the thickness of the button.

All buttons are U.S., unless otherwise stated.

One of the more common, and totally wonderful characteristics of these buttons are the heavy metal loop shanks. Many of these buttons were used on coats, so the shanks needed to be large enough to fit through the heavy fabrics. Consequently, in my opinion, this fine workmanship is the reason so many of these buttons have survived in good condition.

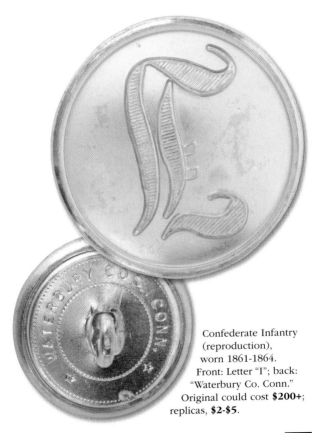

Confederate Infantry
(reproduction),
worn 1861-1864.
Front: Letter "I"; back:
"Waterbury Co. Conn."
Original could cost **$200+**;
replicas, **$2-$5**.

Infantry, Continental, Army, General Service, 1777-1786. Original was cast pewter. This copy is brass with no back marks. Original **$200+**; replicas, **$2-$5**.

Army, circa 1820-1840. Great coat button. Front: flying eagle above initials U.S, wreath below; back: "United States" separated by stars. Heavy brass shank suggests authenticity; however, research states this button had no back mark? **$75+**.

Infantry officer, 1851-
1902, two-piece
construction. Front:
eagle with shield,
containing letter I.
Variations exist; back:
"Horstmann Bros &
Co./Phila," which dates
this button between 1859-
1863, **$10**.

General service, 1854-1902. Front: This eagle has a shield that does not contain a letter. It was used for enlisted personnel for all services in 1854; back: "Horstmann Bros & Co./Phila" two-piece construction, **$3**.

Artillery, 1855-1902.
Front: Eagle with shield
containing letter "A":
back: "Superior Quality,"
$6.

Cavalry, 1855-1902.
Front: Eagle with shield
containing letter "C"; back:
"Shannon Miller & Crane
N.Y." dates button to 1865-
1892, **$6**.

Rifles, 1821-1854.
Front: Eagle with shield
containing letter "R";
back: "WM. H. Smith" dates
button as 1845, **$15**.

Army, general staff, 1832-1902. This button is of three-piece construction, having a separate rim that holds the front and back together. Front: This style eagle was used until 1902, when it changed to the present style; back: "J.M. Litchfield & Co S.F. Cal" dates button between 1880-1895, **$3**.

Army, general service, 1902 to 1918, WWI, brass, two-piece construction. Front: The Great Seal of The United States; used on all buttons after 1902 to present. Back: "J R Gaunt & Son Ltd, London, Eng," **$3**.

Army, general service,
1902-1918, WWI, copper,
two-piece construction.
Front: Great Seal; back:
"U.S. Army Standard," **$3**.

Army, general service,
1902-1918, WWI, brass,
two-piece construction.
Front: variation of earlier
seal; back: "Horstmann/
Phila," **$2**.

Army, general service, 1902-1918, WWI, bronze, two-piece construction. Front: Great Seal; back: "C. Kenyon Co. New York," **$5**.

Army, general service,
1902-1918, WWI,
vegetable ivory, one piece.
Front: Great Seal; back:
brass shank, no marks, **$5**.

Army, general service,
1902-1918, WWI,
oil cloth, two-piece
construction. Front: Great
Seal; no back mark, **$5**.

Army, general service, 1902-1945, WWII, bronze, two-piece construction. Front: Great Seal; back: "Horstmann"; there is more, but it is too worn to read, **$3**.

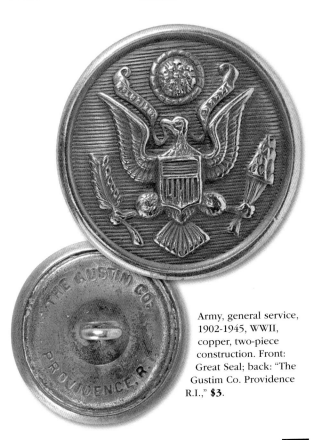

Army, general service, 1902-1945, WWII, copper, two-piece construction. Front: Great Seal; back: "The Gustim Co. Providence R.I.," **$3**.

Army, general service,
1902-1945, WWII,
brass, two-piece
construction. Front:
Great Seal; back: "Rex
Products Corp. New
Rochelle N.Y.," **$2**.

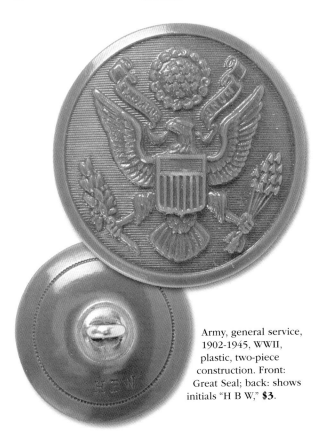

Army, general service, 1902-1945, WWII, plastic, two-piece construction. Front: Great Seal; back: shows initials "H B W," **$3**.

Army, general service,
1945 to present, brass,
two-piece construction.
Front: Great Seal; back:
"Waterbury Button Co.
Conn.," **$3**.

Army Air Corp, WWII, brass, two-piece construction. Front: wings with propeller; back: no marks, self-shank, **$4**.

Army Corp of Engineers.
This distinctive design has
been on buttons since about
1814 and it is the only
branch to never change
its design. Front: The eagle
holds a banner with the word
"Essayons" (We Try); the eagle
flies over water with a sun and
fortress in the background. Back:
"Scovill Mf'g Co. Waterbury," which
dates this button to 1850 to 1865, **$5**.

US Air Force, 1947-1995, white metal, two-piece construction. Front: shield with eagle and 13 stars; back: "Waterbury Button Co., Conn.," **$2**.

US Air Force, 1947-
1955, brass, two-
piece construction,
back marked, **$1**.

US Air Force, 1995 to present, white metal, two-piece construction. Front: star with wings; back: "Waterbury Co's. Conn. W 21," **$2**.

US Marines,
1821 to present,
plastic (possibly composition),
one-piece construction with
inserted metal loop shank.
Front: all Marine buttons
depict an eagle perched
on the stock of a slanted
anchor, with 13 stars (15
stars also exist) at the top of
the circle. Lined background.
Back: no back marks, **$2**.

US Marines, copper, two-piece construction; back: back mark is not clear, **$3**.

US Marines, bronze, two-piece construction; back: "Scovill Mf'g Co., **$3**.

US Marines, copper, two-piece construction, back: "J.C.L. Shabeck. Prov. R.I.," **$4**.

US Marines, bronze, two-piece construction, small sleeve button, back: "Art Metal Works" and more, which is unreadable, **$2**.

US Navy, steel, two-piece construction. Front: anchor with rope, NAVY at top; back: unmarked, **$2**.

US Navy, plastic (composition), one-piece construction, inserted metal shank, newer version of previous button, **$1**.

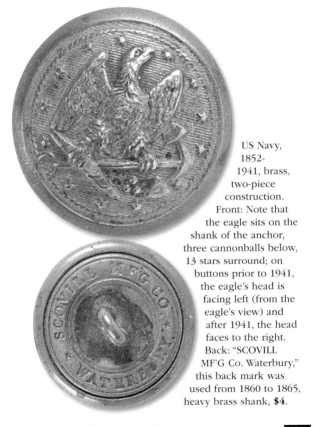

US Navy, 1852-1941, brass, two-piece construction. Front: Note that the eagle sits on the shank of the anchor, three cannonballs below, 13 stars surround; on buttons prior to 1941, the eagle's head is facing left (from the eagle's view) and after 1941, the head faces to the right. Back: "SCOVILL MF'G Co. Waterbury," this back mark was used from 1860 to 1865, heavy brass shank, **$4**.

US Navy, 1941-present,
brass, two-piece
construction, heavy
brass shank. Front: eagle
faces right; back: "Superior
Quality," **$2**.

US Navy, 1941-present,
plastic, one piece,
inserted metal loop
shank, no back mark, **$2**.

US Navy, 1830-1852, brass, two-piece construction. Front: the eagle sits on the stock of the anchor, head to the right, encircled by 13 stars; back: no marks, **$8**.

US Navy, pea coat button, four-hole sew-through; this style was made in hard rubber, as well as composition (plastic). There is no back mark on this button, and therefore it is composition and probably manufactured between 1910 and 1930, **$3**.

US Navy, overcoat button, four-hole sew-through, post 1900. This design replaced the earlier version with the stars and these are still in use today but made from plastic, **$2**.

US Navy, small version of overcoat button, used on dress blues pants, plastic, **50 cents**.

US Coast Guard, post 1915, brass, two-piece construction. Front: an eagle on the stock of an anchor, a wreath below; back: "Vanguard Corp. New York," **$2**.

US Naval Reserve, brass, two-piece construction, button was worn by chief petty officers. Front: anchor; back: "Waterbury Button Co." with three stars; this back mark appears from 1849-1965, **$2**.

New York National Guard, brass, two-piece construction; front: numeral "23," "Vigilantia" above and "N.G.S.N.Y." below; the number stands for the 23rd regiment. Back: "Waterbury Button Co.," **$5**.

Military Academy uniform button, brass, two-piece construction. Front: fox; back: "Superior Quality," **$4**. The school was located in the Los Angeles area, but I have not been able to identify it exactly.

US Military Academy, West Point, N.Y., one of the earlier buttons worn by cadets, founded in 1802, two-piece construction. This button has been dated 1923 (records). Front: cadet, U.S.M.A., eagle. Back: no marks, **$3**.

US Post Office, brass, three-piece construction, circa 1850-1865. Front: "N Y P O" above a rider on horseback, P O D beneath. This seal was adopted in 1837. Buttons are often found "stock" with just POD. Back: "Scovill Mf'g Co Waterbury," **$6**.

Santa Fe Railroad, white metal, two-piece construction, chartered in Feb 1859, The Atchison, Topeka, and Santa Fe railroad, often just "Santa Fe," ceased to be when it merged with the Burlington Northern Railroad, Dec. 31, 1996. Front: Santa Fe on a cross within a circle; back: "Superior Quality," **$3**.

Chicago City Police, brass, two-piece construction. Front: The city's seal; back: "Superior Quality," **$8**.

St. Louis & San
Francisco Railway,
commonly referred to
as the Frisco. Formed
on Sept. 7, 1876, this
railroad line underwent
several reformations
before being acquired
by Burlington Northern
RR on Nov. 21, 1980. Front:
Frisco; back: "A.G. Meier &
Co. Chicago, Ill," **$3**.

Motorman, "stock" button used by many railroads, buttons with pullman, conductor, etc. were also made. Back: "Scovill Mf'g Co. Waterbury," 1850-1865, **$1**.

Grand Army of the Republic (GAR), powerful veterans organization formed in 1866 for honorably discharged veterans of the union service branches. Front: many variations in the shape and look of the letters exist and this button is a rather rare and fine example, with the "A" being more pointed, rather than square at the top; back: "Scoville Mf'g Co. Waterbury," **$10**. More common GAR buttons are **$3-$8**. GAR was instrumental in founding Memorial Day as a national holiday and setting up services for veterans. The last meeting was held in Indiana in 1949 and the last member, Albert Woolson, died in 1956 at the age of 109.

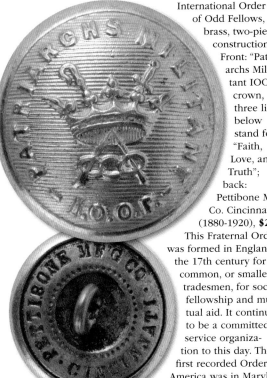

International Order of Odd Fellows, brass, two-piece construction. Front: "Patriarchs Militant IOOF" crown, three links below stand for "Faith, Love, and Truth"; back: Pettibone Mf'g Co. Cincinnati" (1880-1920), **$2**. This Fraternal Order was formed in England in the 17th century for the common, or smaller tradesmen, for social fellowship and mutual aid. It continues to be a committed service organization to this day. The first recorded Order in America was in Maryland in 1819.

US Lighthouse Service, white metal, two-piece construction. Front: lighthouse; back: "Cheshire Button CT. USA," **$4**. This is a new button (2000) and they can be purchased at lighthouse museums and Web sites.

State seal buttons were worn by many US militia companies in the 1800s and they bear a design based on the state seal. Newer buttons were later produced for collectors, so look closely. The more exact the design, the newer the button (in most cases). Many people try to collect all 50 state buttons.

Missouri, 1821; back: "Pettibone Bros. Mfg Co," **$5**.

New Jersey; back: "Waterbury
Button Co Conn," **$5**.

Rhode Island; back:
"Ridabock & Co New York"
(1880-1940), **$8**.

Fire Department, stock, white metal, two-piece construction; back: "Extra Quality," **$2**.

San Francisco Fire
Department, white metal,
two-piece construction; back:
"Waterbury Button Co," **$10**.

Boy Scouts of America were founded in 1910 as an extension of the scouting movement in England by Lord Robert Baden-Powell.

Boy Scouts of America uniform button, metal over mold, two-piece, four-hole sew-through. Front: "Boy Scouts of America"; back: unmarked, **50 cents**.

Boy Scouts uniform button, metal, two-piece with shank. Front: wolf head, "Cubs BSA," and a paw; back: "Sweet Orr Uniforms," **$1**.

Boy Scouts uniform button, metal, two-piece with shank. Front: eagle insignia with motto "Be Prepared" beneath; back: marked, but very worn, **$1**.

Boy Scouts, plastic with metal eagle insignia in center, two-hole sew-through, **$1**.

Girl Scouts were founded by Juliette "Daisy" Gordon Low on March 12, 1912. The division into Brownies, Intermediate and Senior came about in the 1930s.

Brownie Girl Scouts uniform button, vegetable ivory, circa 1950s, **75 cents**.

Girl Scouts uniform button, vegetable ivory, circa 1950s, **$1**.

Vegetable Ivory

Vegetable Ivory (VI) is such a strange name, considering that VI buttons are made from neither vegetable or ivory. VI is actually a nut that comes from a palm tree in South America. The nut is called either tagua or corzo and has a dense meaty center. The nuts are sliced and shaped into buttons and designs are either carved or impressed into the surface. Often the buttons are left natural and the beautiful ivory color is seen. Because the nuts are so dense they only take

These slices will soon be buttons.

dye on the surface of the button. When the designs and shanks are carved, the ivory color shows through. The shanks are a tunnel-style self-shank.

On occasion, the buttons are dyed after they are carved. VI buttons were a staple button for a long time, peaking between 1870 and 1920. Because they were inexpensive to produce, and took design easily, they were a favorite for uniform buttons. Boy and

Girl Scout buttons were made from VI. They were durable and stood up to wear and light wash, but over time they began to "craze" and fall apart. This is due to moisture (after all, moisture causes the nuts to fall off the trees in the Rain Forest) and also due to their organic nature. This "crazing" can also help you identify a VI button.

It is because of this deterioration that water is not the best way to clean your VI buttons. A careful buff with a polishing cloth or a drop of baby oil (dry thoroughly) is all you need to make these buttons shine.

Because these buttons are fairly common, be on the lookout for less common types, like pictorials, OMEs and larger sizes. Remember to look at the back for that tell-tale shank style (on most).

These buttons have heavy crazing marks.

VI, very small, self-shank, raised center with an incised design, **75 cents**.

VI, small, two-hole sew-through, the front of this button has a typical impressed line design, **50 cents**.

VI, small, self-shank,
typical VI button with
impressed geometric
design, **50 cents**.
Notice the ivory color
where the shank was
drilled out but the dye did
not penetrate.

VI, small, self-shank,
lovely natural coloring
with radiating circles
impressed in the center,
50 cents.

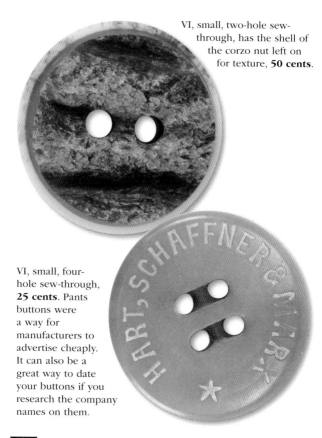

VI, small, two-hole sew-through, has the shell of the corzo nut left on for texture, **50 cents**.

VI, small, four-hole sew-through, **25 cents**. Pants buttons were a way for manufacturers to advertise cheaply. It can also be a great way to date your buttons if you research the company names on them.

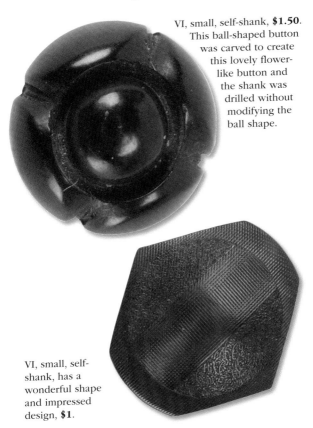

VI, small, self-shank, **$1.50**. This ball-shaped button was carved to create this lovely flower-like button and the shank was drilled without modifying the ball shape.

VI, small, self-shank, has a wonderful shape and impressed design, **$1**.

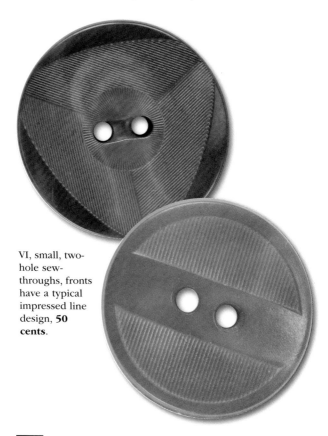

VI, small, two-hole sew-throughs, fronts have a typical impressed line design, **50 cents**.

VI, small, machine-pierced designs, black dyed button is a
two-hole sew-through and the other two have cylindrical self-
shanks, **$2** each.

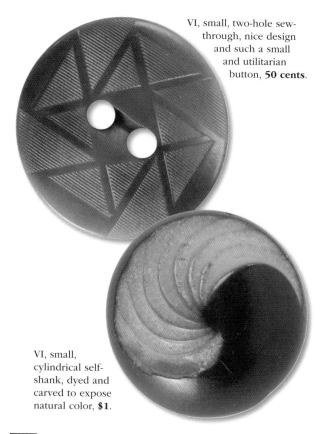

VI, small, two-hole sew-through, nice design and such a small and utilitarian button, **50 cents**.

VI, small, cylindrical self-shank, dyed and carved to expose natural color, **$1**.

VI, small, two-hole sew-through, dyed and carved to expose the natural color of the nut, **$1**.

VI, small, whistle, raised center, border has incised pattern, **$1**.

VI, small, two-hole sew-through, dyed and carved design, **75 cents**.

VI, small, pin shank, thick disc of carved VI, steel-cut center and metal OME, harder to find, **$13**.

VI, medium, self-shank, especially nice impressed design, **$1**.

VI, medium, self-shank, especially nice impressed design, **$1**.

VI, medium, self-shank, 13 stars and anchor suggest this could be a Navy uniform button, but I found no evidence of this. Still, it is a nice button, **$2**.

VI, medium, self-shank, carved and dyed twice, more modern design, **$1.50**.

VI, medium, metal loop shank, VI disk with metal OME berries, lovely button, **$13**.

VI, 3/4" long, whistle, impressed and lovely design, unusual shape, **$1**.

VI, medium, whistle, plain but polished, great button, **75 cents**.

Woods

The use of woods for buttons is centuries old. Unfortunately, most old wooden buttons did not survive, due to natural deterioration and use. Wood was often used as a base button, which was covered with fabric, crochet or other fibers. These buttons are listed as fabric buttons. As you will see from the buttons shown in this chapter, wood is a versatile medium and it was used in many different ways when creating buttons.

Most wood buttons can be identified by their grain lines. While not common, look for back marks. Some wood buttons may have initials such as "ANN" or "GAP." They should never be cleaned with water; a clean polishing cloth is the best cleaning tool.

Wood, set in metal rim, two-hole sew-through, **50 cents**.

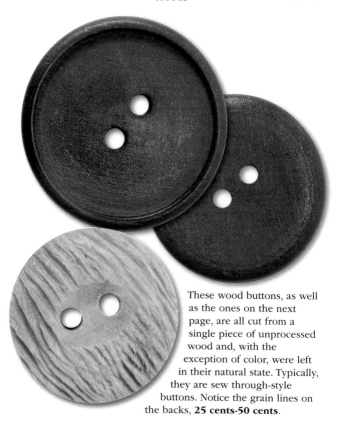

These wood buttons, as well as the ones on the next page, are all cut from a single piece of unprocessed wood and, with the exception of color, were left in their natural state. Typically, they are sew through-style buttons. Notice the grain lines on the backs, **25 cents-50 cents**.

Wood, carved with a
plastic embellishment,
metal loop shank, not quite
so typical, $4.

Wood, burned design, sew-through, newer button, **75 cents-$1**.

Wood, burned design, sew-through, newer button, **75 cents-$1**.

Wood, appears to be unprocessed, with self, channel-style shank, front of the button has a simple pressed design in the center, **$1.50**.

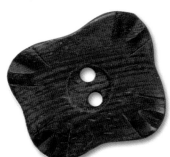

Wood, unprocessed, two-hole sew-through, burned design with nice shape, new (JHB), **$1.30**.

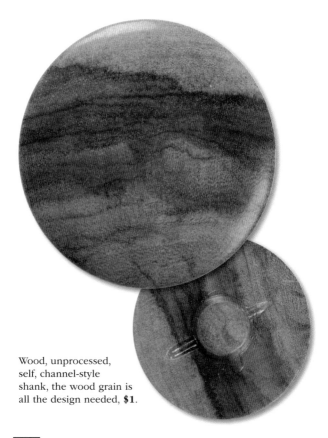

Wood, unprocessed,
self, channel-style
shank, the wood grain is
all the design needed, **$1**.

Warman's Buttons Field Guide

Wood, unprocessed and carved, applied plastic shank, horse, new (JHB), **$1**.

Wood, novelty buttons (JHB), some are made of thin, unprocessed and dye-cut wood, accented with burned designs; others are constructed from inlaid veneers; sew-through or applied plastic shanks, **$1** each.

Wood, large acorn shape, two-hole
sew-through, early 1900s, **$5**.

Syroco or Burwood, wood composition, constructed from molded processed wood pulp, two-hole sew-through, 1920s, painted, depicts "Trees, House with Portico and Carriage," **$30+**. No back marks appear on these buttons, but they were most likely made by the Syroco or Burwood companies and therefore referred to by these two names.

Syroco or Burwood,
wood composition,
two-hole sew-through,
painted with floral design,
1920s, **$5**.

Metal with wood
background, listed as a
wood button/background,
$10-$15.

Wood, carved, large, metal loop shank inserted, **$4**. This is one of my favorites!

Wood, medium, toggle-style
button with staple-type shank,
new, JHB, **$1**.

Wood, medium, applied metal plate shank, "studio" button by artist Kay Ferguson, one in a series of lighthouse buttons, **$5-$15**. On the front is a laser-carved image of the Coquille lighthouse in Bandon, Oregon; the back is signed and dated, with location of lighthouse, "Bandon, Ore. Kay '96."

Others

This chapter covers button materials such as leather, bone and antler, hoof and horn, and coconut shell. These buttons were common and durable, and often made as a side industry. The materials were plentiful and easy to work with.

Bone, antler, hoof and horn

Bone, antler, hoof and horn buttons are often found in their natural form, being sliced and polished. Horn tips are commonly used for toggle buttons. Leftover scraps are often ground and powdered and then molded.

In the early 1800s, thin sheets of horn and hoof were heated, molded and dyed to produce lovely buttons. Hoof and horn buttons often have a small hole in the back. This "pick" mark is where the button was removed from the mold with a sharp pick. Also, hoof and horn buttons, when held to the light, appear transparent.

To clean these buttons, use a soft cloth and a touch of mineral oil. Dry thoroughly.

Coconut shell

Coconut shell was used to make buttons mainly for the tourist trade, but they have been commercially made for the garment industry as of late.

While they can be cleaned with water, you may want to use a polishing cloth or a small amount of mineral oil to keep them from looking dull and drying out.

Leather

Leather buttons have been made from animal skins of all sorts, from cows and reptiles to fish and stingrays. They take dye well and can be embossed, stamped or tooled in design.

These buttons can be fragile, and rotting buttons should be thrown out, as they can infect your collection. A damp cloth can be used for cleaning but be certain the buttons are completely dry before storing them. Leather cleaners and conditioners should be used sparingly.

Bone, large, two-hole sew-through, stained with carved design, newer button (JHB), **$3**.

Bone, medium, two-hole sew-through, carved design, newer
button, **$2**.

Bone, small, two-hole sew-through, typical bone
underwear button, note the large holes, these buttons
are plentiful, **50 cents**.

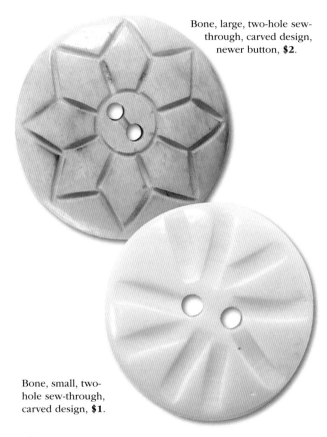

Bone, large, two-hole sew-through, carved design, newer button, **$2**.

Bone, small, two-hole sew-through, carved design, **$1**.

Hoof, small, two-hole sew-through, unusual realistic shape, **$2**.

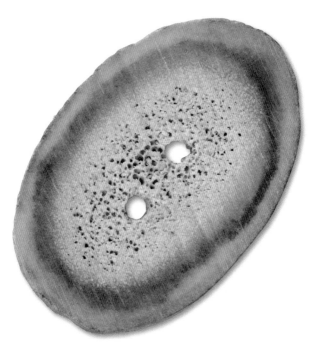

Caribou antler, medium, two-hole sew-through, sliced and left natural, note the tiny holes in the center marrow area, **$2**.

Coconut shell, small, two-hole sew-through, new button, **25 cents**.

Coconut shell, medium,
applied plastic shank,
new (JHB) novelty
buttons, **$1**.

Leather, small, prong-
style shank, front has a
metal horse head and a
stamped border, **$3**.

Leather, small, metal loop shank,
stitched edge, **$1**.

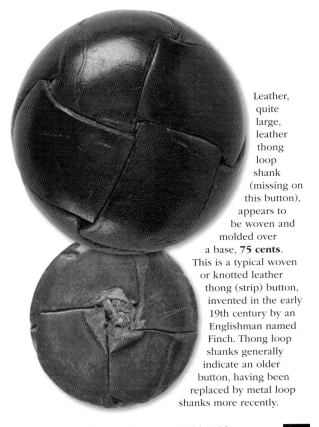

Leather, quite large, leather thong loop shank (missing on this button), appears to be woven and molded over a base, **75 cents**. This is a typical woven or knotted leather thong (strip) button, invented in the early 19th century by an Englishman named Finch. Thong loop shanks generally indicate an older button, having been replaced by metal loop shanks more recently.

Leather, medium,
leather thong loop
shank, dyed black,
another typical thong-
style button, **25 cents**.

Leather, medium, newer leather thong button with metal loop shank, lovely shape, **75 cents**.

Leather, medium, two-piece covered button, with metal back and shank, leather is in good condition, **50 cents**.

Leather, small, two-hole
sew-through, embossed
leather over metal frame,
50 cents.

Leather, small, two-hole
sew-through, stamped
design, **50 cents**.

Leather, medium, metal loop shank with plastic plate back, back mark "Hemisphere," front is molded leather to imitate woven strips, **$1**.

Metal, medium, two-
piece construction,
knob-like shank with
four holes punched in
the sides, as well as one
in the center. This button
imitates leather, **50 cents**.

Leather, medium, two-hole sew-through, leather over wood mold, **$1**. Appears to be solid, but a study of the inside of the holes, as well as the sharp tapping noise against a hard surface, reveals otherwise.

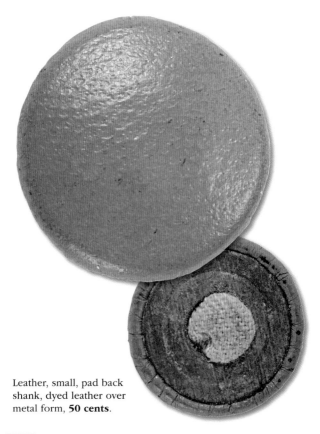

Leather, small, pad back
shank, dyed leather over
metal form, **50 cents**.

Leather, medium,
plastic shank, thin
leather over plastic
mold, lovely attempt to
make a new button look
old and detailed, **75 cents**.

Plastic, small, metal loop shank, **50 cents**. This button is another good look-a-like and a close look at the shank area shows where the surface was applied.

Glossary

These definitions are taken from the National Button Society's 2008 Classification Guide, unless otherwise stated.

Back mark: Maker's name, brand, patent quality mark, etc. May be verbal or pictorial in nature.

Bubble top: Similar to a tight top except that there is discernible air space under the sheet of celluloid.

Collet: A metal band or collar.

Crazed: Minute cracks produced in or on the surface or glaze of a button.

Decorative finish (DF): A surface treatment or coating. Examples include paint, luster, and frosted.

Four-way metal shank: A shank type found on glass buttons. It is a hollow metal cube with four holes (one on each side of the cube) through which a needle and thread may pass.

Glows: A bubble top that has a completely or partly transparent bubble that reveals a base of foil, iridescent celluloid or other shiny material.

Impressed: The top surface of the button design appears ground, or polished smooth, the part surrounding being sharply sunk.

Incised: A method of working a design, which creates a very fine line.

Inkwell: Refers to a china button center that is relatively deep.

Kiddie buttons: Small non-realistic glass or plastic buttons made for children's wear with pictorial designs of children's themes (no fruit or flower designs). May have painted or transfer design.

Lacy or lacy-like: Glass buttons (pre 1918) having a delicate molded surface design. These buttons appear to be made by placing tiny individual pieces on the buttons surface. Lacy-like refers to modern buttons with this type of design.

Luster: A metallic decorative finish.

Moonglow (not NBS): A glass button that has a clear layer of glass over the color layer, giving it a sort of bubble through which the color layer is seen.

OME (Other Material Embellishment): Material(s) different from the base (of the button) added onto or inlaid into the surface during or after formation of the button to enhance the face design. Examples include pearl pieces, cut steel or rhinestones.

Omega shank (not NBS): A shank type commonly found on celluloid buttons, it is shaped like the Greek letter "omega."

Pierced: Holes or openings that have been cut or drilled through the body of the button from the front completely to the back. Other terms for this type of design include "openwork" and "filigree."

Pressed: A shallow surface design created through heat and pressure. Applies to materials such as wood, celluloid and vegetable ivory.

Realistic: Button has the shape of and depicts/ resembles (an actual object). Buttons made from the actual object (sea shell, coin, etc.) do not apply.

Self shank (not NBS): A button shank that is formed as part of the buttons construction, as opposed to a shank that is added separately or inserted into the back of the button.

Sets vs. Series: A set is typically three or more non-identical buttons (with a common theme) sold on the same card commercially, made of the same material, decorated in like manner. Color is often a factor to the relation of the set. Series of buttons are groups of related realistics, sold on separate cards and sequentially. An example of a series is the JHB Beatrix Potter buttons shown on pages 318-319.

Studio buttons: Buttons designed and fabricated primarily, but not exclusively, for sale to button collectors. They are not mass produced, but are made in limited quantities and express the artist's creativity.

Buttons should be labeled as to maker and date when possible.

Tight top: A solid sheet of celluloid drawn tightly and smoothly over the button frame. Usually, although not always, a metal band clamps the celluloid to the back.

Tunnel shank (not NBS): A shank style commonly found on celluloid buttons, they are domed and have the appearance of a railroad tunnel for a model train set.

Twinkles: Metal button. Two- and/or three-piece construction. Face is perforated with holes, slots, or filigree and backed with shiny liners that twinkle when illuminated. Liners are usually gold or silver (iridescent and colored liners are less common). Any amount of reflective material is acceptable, i.e. backgrounds, borders, or a small section of the design (like a window).

Watch wheel: Metal embellishment in the form of a cog, gear, or other wheel like object resembling those found in a watch works. Often found on shell or glass buttons.

Whistle: A type of sew-through button, of solid or hollow construction, with a vertical hole on the front (small in diameter) and two or more holes on the back. Button holes are not fully visible from the top of the button.

Resources

I can be reached through my Web site, **www. JillionsofButtons.com.**

Here are other sources of information:

Button clubs

One of the most satisfying things I did when I began collecting and researching buttons was to join my local button club. Like most people I know, I was completely unaware that such a group existed. Actually, it turns out that there is a National Button Society with a membership of over 3,000 collectors worldwide. In addition to the national society, many states have a society, with local clubs supporting the state chapter. There is even a cyber club you can join. You can belong to clubs at any or all levels. Many collectors belong to multiple state societies, which may sound crazy, but there are advantages.

For starters, dues are extremely inexpensive; as little as $25 per year at the national level. Local club dues are as little as $3 per year. Each state society, as well as the national society, publishes a bulletin containing informative articles written by the membership that cover fascinating historical stories related to buttons, in-depth information about various types of buttons and gorgeous pictures of other people's wonderful collections. Each bulletin is sure to inspire and teach every level of collector. The more clubs you are a member of, the more access you will have to untold knowledge. In addition, the NBS and most state societies have a yearly show where there are informative seminars, buttons to studied and purchased, new friends to make and incredible competitions.

I first learned of the existence of the societies when I attended the spring show sponsored by the Colorado State Button Society. I knew I wanted to learn more about buttons, but I wasn't prepared for what I experienced at this show. There were button trays (buttons mounted to special mat boards) mounted on easels as far as the eye could see in the large banquet room. To say I saw buttons is like saying the Hope Diamond is a rock. I never imagined that such beautiful things were created for the simple task of fastening clothing. As button collectors are fond of saying, I was "bitten by the button bug." I learned when and where my local button club met and I joined immediately.

Button club members are generous with their knowledge, time, friendship, and sometimes even their buttons. I am privileged and blessed to know them, and I could never have completed this book without them. I hope that you will find your button experiences to be as fulfilling as mine continue to be. Button up!

Other resources

The Internet is such a wonderful tool to the collector. You can access the NBS Web site, **www.nationalbuttonsociety.org**, which has links to state and local button club sites, shows, and other up-to-date information on collecting buttons. I previously mentioned the bulletins that are sent to members and you can order back issues of these, as well as other informative NBS publications about buttons. Many respected button dealers also have Web sites. Many are linked to the NBS site or can be found advertising in the back of the bulletin. One of my favorites (and I have many) is **www.buttonimages.com** by Lisa Schulz. In addition to button sales (online and at shows), this site has a fantastic section about cleaning buttons and another section about identifying them. She also sells tools, including brass brushes.

Another of the invaluable perks that may be available to many button club members at the state level is the ability to borrow books and learning resources from the society's library. Many groups have large collections available and since many resource books are out of print, this can be an invaluable tool.

Your local library is another great resource for information. There are several books that I would consider standards for your research or for your personal library. I have listed these in the bibliography so that you will have all the necessary information. There are some drawbacks I should mention, however. One problem is age. Many books are either out of print or out of date. Some of these books have been revised and reprinted, and they are still viable references, as long as you do not take any values listed to be current. Another problem you may have is the cost of some of the books. One of the most referenced books by collectors is *The Big Book of Buttons* by Elizabeth Hughes and Marion Lester. This comprehensive volume is being updated (for the 3rd time) and the button world is very excited about it. Many collectors are selling their older copies so shop around because I found them listed on Amazon. com for $412 to $625. While this book is a must have for the serious collector, there are many other titles that are informative and keep money in your wallet to buy buttons with.

Speaking of Amazon, you might check out sites such as this for books and sites like eBay for books and buttons. After careful research, you can make educated purchases that you will enjoy for a lifetime.

Bibliography

Books

Osborne, Peggy Ann. *Button Button Identification & Price Guide*, Schiffer Publishing, Ltd., Pennsylvania, 1993.

Wisniewski, Debra J. *Antique & Collectible Buttons Identification & Values*, Collector Books, Kentucky. 1997.

Hughes, Elizabeth and Lester, Marion. *The Big Book of Buttons*, New Leaf Publishers, Maine. First printing, 1981. Second printing, 1991. (1991 also the copyright date.)

Booklet/Publication

Weingarten, Lucille and Speights, *M.W. Modern West German Glass Buttons 2002*. A National Button Society Publication.

National Button Society. *Official NBS Classification 2008 Awards*.

National Button Society. *Beginner's Booklet*.

Online Articles

"Identifying and Testing for Materials," www. buttonimages.com, revised 11/25/2000, written by Lisa Schulz.

"Cleaning and Restoring Buttons," www. buttonimages.com, revised 4/07, copyrighted 1998.

Savor Timeless Stitches

Warman's® Vintage Quilts
Identification and Price Guide
by Maggi McCormick Gordon

This beautifully illustrated and inspiring book contains fascinating colors, fabrics, designs and handiwork, all used to celebrate 300+ quilts, produced between 1850 and 1960. Divided clearly into to specific categories, this book features:

- Patchwork Quilts – Divided into eight subcategories including Log Cabin, Representational Blocks, Curves
- Applique – Featuring two subcategories in Sunbonnet Sue and Pictorials and Florals
- Embellished Quilts – Showcasing Embroidered Quilts and Crazy Quilts
- Small Quilts – Categorized as Crib of Doll quilts
- Non-traditional Quilts – Reflected in African-American and Siddi quilts

Softcover • 8-1/4 x 10-7/8 • 256 pages • 350 color photos
Item# Z2267 • $24.99